JOSCELINE DIMBLEBY'S

Book of Puddings
Desserts and Savouries

"I sing the sweets I know, the charm I feel —
My morning incense, and my evening meal."

Joel Barlow, 1754–1812

By the same author
A TASTE OF DREAMS

JOSCELINE DIMBLEBY'S
Book of Puddings Desserts and Savouries

 HODDER AND STOUGHTON
LONDON SYDNEY AUCKLAND TORONTO

British Library Cataloguing in Publication Data
Dimbleby, Josceline
Josceline Dimbleby's Book of Puddings Desserts and
Savouries

1. Desserts
I. Book of Puddings, desserts and savouries
641.8'6   TX773

ISBN 0 340 23720 1

INTRODUCTION

"Kissing don't last: cookery do!"
George Meredith, 1828–1909

"Cooks are Mortals Divine."
Voltaire, 1694–1778

Who is not a little disappointed when a delicious, thoughtfully cooked meal ends abruptly with no pudding, no surprise or treat to complete the happy occasion?

Yet puddings have been out of fashion. After the war, few people could afford cooks any more. The modern woman set about her new domestic duties bravely, but when it came to the pudding or desert she was defeated. Cheese and fruit had to do. Now the style is changing—not least because fresh fruit and cheese have become so expensive, and diets no longer have the cachet they once had. People are learning not to starve, but to eat less, to eat more sensibly and to take more exercise, so that once again they can allow themselves the occasional mouthwatering pudding.

Cooking has become much more popular over the last few years and people want to try things they wouldn't have bothered with before. As the cost of ingredients goes up and up, they seem to be learning how best to make use of them and this develops their culinary imagination. Now that it is impossible and expensive to entertain friends at a restaurant, learning to cook well creatively is so much more important. And then there is competition. More and more housewives are becoming good cooks and of course they want to impress their rivals. Few dishes can be as exciting and impressive as a successful pudding.

The last course is the moment to whet the jaded appetite and end the meal with a flourish, an important moment, but one at which many a good cook's inspiration sadly fails. Remember that, free from the more conventional demands of the main course, the pudding or dessert is your chance to add a touch of real imagination or fantasy to your meal—colour, shape, texture and decoration can really come into their own.

At weekends the family will feel Sunday lunch to be much more of a special occasion if they are presented with a beautiful home-made pudding. Who can resist an old favourite like Apple Pie or Queen of Puddings? During

INTRODUCTION

the grey, dull, winter days a piping hot old-fashioned pudding will cheer people up immeasurably, while the variety of glamorous and mouthwatering concoctions to be put together with summer fruits is endless. It's also fun to try the sweets with cooking traditions very different from our own. A success using what seem to us to be bizarre methods and odd combinations of flavours can lead one to a whole new line of dishes.

This book is not supposed to be a book of basic puddings, recipes for which can be found in all the good cookery manuals. It is simply a varied collection of my favourite recipes, mostly original ones, I trust, but also those that I have found to be the best versions of the old favourites, so I hope it will provide an easy answer when next you say, "I just can't think what to have for pudding!" Although I admit to having an incurably sweet tooth which of course makes me predisposed towards puddings, I realise that not everyone feels quite the same greedy enthusiasm. But I still believe that a meal should not tail off, that it should have a proper finale. So, for confirmed pudding haters, I have included a few savouries. These seem to have faded out of fashion even more than puddings, yet they can be the little chef-d'oeuvres of the meal.

Please don't think that I am advocating puddings for every meal—we would all get far too fat. They should be kept as a treat for weekends and holidays, and as the perfect end to a dinner party. Because puddings are a luxury there is a wicked feeling of indulgence about them and they are therefore more pleasure to make than everyday food.

I'm afraid that while I was writing this book my family was somewhat overloaded with puddings—two or even three puddings could appear at any one meal. I remember my husband, trying hard to stick to a strict diet, opening the fridge one day to look for a stick of celery or a hunk of cheese and crying out in despair that he could find nothing, absolutely nothing, but shelf after shelf laden with puddings!

CONTENTS

ILLUSTRATIONS

List of Colour Plates

Author's Note
In all the recipes using eggs I have used large (Size 1 or 2), so if you only have
small ones, use more.

All the recipes will feed approximately six people unless otherwise stated,
though as a good pudding is something of which one is apt to have two, or
sometimes shamefully even three helpings, I have made the quantities
generous. So you could reckon that mostly they will satisfy six very greedy
people, eight normal ones and perhaps even ten more modest eaters!

FAMILY FAVOURITES

Apples in Ambush

There must be more ways to cook apples than any other fruit, which is very necessary in the autumn if you have any apple trees in your garden. Here is a rather delicious pudding with a slightly sharp, mousse-like top.

1–1½ lb cooking apples (450–700 g)
1 teaspoonful cinnamon
2 rounded tablespoonfuls soft
brown sugar
1 oz butter (25 g)
grated rind and juice of 1 small lemon
2 oz fresh white breadcrumbs (50 g)
2 oz castor sugar (50 g)
1 carton soured cream
3 large eggs – separated
¼ teaspoonful cream of tartar

Butter a 2½–3-pint (1½–1¾-litre) ovenproof dish. Peel and core the apples and slice very thinly. Arrange the slices on the bottom of the dish and sprinkle with the cinnamon and brown sugar. Dot with the butter and, reserving the grated lemon rind, add the lemon juice. Put the breadcrumbs into a mixing bowl with the castor sugar, the soured cream, the egg yolks and the reserved lemon rind. Stir well together. Heat the oven to Gas Mark 5/375°F. Whisk the egg whites with the cream of tartar until they stand in peaks and then, using a metal spoon, fold lightly into the yolk mixture. Pour on top of the apples and cook in the centre of the oven for about 40 minutes until well risen and brown. Serve hot or cold with cream.

Orange and Apple Surprise

This is a good pudding for all the family. Toffeeish apples are covered by a fresh orange mixture which forms a rich custard with the lightest sponge top.

1 lb cooking apples (450 g)
4 oz butter or margarine (110 g)
1 heaped tablespoonful soft brown sugar
4 oz castor sugar (110 g)
3 large eggs – separated
grated rind and juice of 2 small oranges
1 heaped tablespoonful self-raising flour
a little over $\frac{1}{4}$ pint milk (150 ml)
$\frac{1}{2}$ teaspoonful cream of tartar

Peel, core and chop the apples into small pieces. Melt 2 oz (50 g) of the butter in a frying pan and stir in the apples and the brown sugar. Fry the apple pieces over a high heat, stirring all the time, for about 2 minutes. Transfer to the bottom of a 7–8 in (18–20 cm) soufflé dish. Allow to cool while you make the top.

Heat the oven to Gas Mark 4/350°F. Beat the remaining 2 oz (50 g) butter with the castor sugar until light and fluffy. Separate the yolks from the whites of the eggs and beat the yolks into the sugar and butter mixture. Gradually beat in the orange rind and juice. Sift in the flour and add the milk slowly, beating thoroughly until the mixture is smooth. Whisk the egg whites with the cream of tartar until they stand in peaks. Gently fold into the orange mixture with a metal spoon. Pour this on top of the apples and bake in the centre of the oven at Gas Mark 4/350°F for 40 minutes. Serve hot or cold.

I don't think this pudding really needs cream unless you are feeling particularly greedy.

Cider Apple Meringue

This layered pudding with its sharp apple base, creamy centre and crisp meringue top is good enough for adults and adored by children, thus making it perfect for a weekend lunch.

2 lb cooking apples (900 g)
just under ½ pint cider (275 ml)
juice of 1 lemon
6 oz granulated sugar (175 g)

FOR THE CUSTARD
1 dessertspoonful castor sugar
3 egg yolks
½ pint single cream (275 ml)
1 teaspoonful vanilla essence
(optional)

FOR THE MERINGUE TOP
3 egg whites
good pinch of cream of tartar or salt
5 oz castor sugar (150 g)

Put the cider, lemon juice and sugar in a saucepan. Peel, core and roughly chop the apples and add them to the liquid. Bring to the boil and simmer until the apples are very mushy – about 10–15 minutes. Pour into an ovenproof dish which the apples should only half fill. Set aside to cool. Heat the oven to Gas Mark 5/370°F.

In a double saucepan or a bowl over a pan of simmering water mix a dessertspoonful of castor sugar, the egg yolks (putting aside the whites in a large bowl), the cream and the essence. Allow to thicken over the gently simmering water, stirring constantly with a wooden spoon. When thick enough to coat the spoon, after 4–6 minutes, take off the heat. Pour slowly on to the apple.

Whisk up the egg whites with the cream of tartar or salt until stiff. Beat in all but a spoonful of the castor sugar. Spoon the meringue on top of the custard. Sprinkle on the remaining sugar and bake towards the top of the oven for 15–20 minutes until brown. Serve hot or cold with or without cream.

Country Rhubarb Gingerbread (serves 8–10)

This is dark and moist with a goo of rhubarb in the middle. It will feed a large crowd of people for a weekend lunch.

4 oz butter or margarine (110 g)
4 oz soft brown sugar (110 g)
2 eggs – lightly whisked
8 oz black treacle (225 g)
2 oz crystallised ginger, chopped
finely (50 g)
1 teaspoonful ground ginger
8 oz plain flour (225 g)
1 level teaspoonful bicarbonate of soda
4 tablespoonfuls milk
1 lb rhubarb – chopped into small
pieces (450 g)
icing sugar

Heat the oven to Gas Mark 3/325°F. Butter a fairly shallow, 2–2½-pint capacity (1–1½ litres) flan or pie dish. Beat the butter until creamy, add the sugar and beat thoroughly. Then beat in the eggs, a little at a time. Now pour in the treacle and beat. To measure the treacle either just use a half 1 lb (450 g) tin put a larger tin on your scales and spoon out the required weight. Stir in the crystallised and ground ginger and, using a metal spoon, fold in the flour. Dissolve the bicarbonate of soda in the milk and stir into the cake mixture. Spoon about half of the mixture into the prepared dish, then sprinkle the rhubarb over and cover with the remaining mixture. Bake in the centre of the oven for 45 minutes, then lay foil on top and turn the oven down to Gas Mark 2/300°F for another 30 minutes. Serve hot or cold with cream, and sieve icing sugar all over the top before serving.

Chocolate Pear Pudding

Buttery pears under a moist and spongy chocolate top make a useful and satisfying hot pudding, which is quick to prepare, for all the family. You can use apples, if you like, but pears go particularly well with chocolate.

FOR THE BATTER
3 oz plain flour (75 g)
1 tablespoonful cocoa
½ level teaspoonful bicarbonate of soda
½ level teaspoonful baking powder
1 rounded teaspoonful ground
cinnamon
pinch of salt
5 oz soft dark brown sugar (150 g)
2 tablespoonfuls golden syrup
1 large egg – lightly beaten
4 tablespoonfuls sunflower or corn oil
4 tablespoonfuls milk

1 lb pears (450 g)
1–2 oz butter (25–50 g)
castor sugar

Butter a 2-pint (1-litre) ovenproof dish. Sift the flour, cocoa, bicarbonate of soda, baking powder, cinnamon and salt into a bowl. Stir in the sugar and then add gradually the golden syrup, the egg, the oil and the milk. Beat well to make a smooth batter. Heat the oven to Gas Mark 3/325°F.

Peel, core and slice the pears thinly. Arrange them in the bottom of the buttered dish, generously sprinkled with castor sugar and dotted with butter. Pour the chocolate batter on top and bake in the centre of the oven for 50–60 minutes, until the top is well risen and springy to touch in the centre. Serve warm with cream.

Yorkshire Pears

Buttery pears with an enriched, dramatically risen, sweet Yorkshire pudding top can't fail to please the family. Of course you can use other fruit in season, if you like. If you put the pudding into the oven as you are starting your first course, the timing should be just about right. If the pudding is ready before you are, turn off the heat but don't open the oven door.

$1\frac{1}{2}$ lb semi-hard pears (700 g)
3 tablespoonfuls soft brown sugar
grated rind of 1 lemon
$1\frac{1}{2}$ oz butter or margarine (40 g)

FOR THE BATTER
$\frac{1}{4}$ pint milk (275 ml)
1 oz butter or margarine (25 g)
$2\frac{1}{2}$ oz self-raising flour (60 g)
1 oz castor sugar (25 g)
2 eggs

Turn the oven to Gas Mark 8/450°F. Peel the pears and cut each one into six slices. Put them into an 8–9 in (20–23 cm) ovenproof bowl, sprinkle on the sugar and lemon rind and dot all over with the butter. Cook in the centre of the oven for 20–30 minutes or until the pears are just soft. Meanwhile prepare the top. Bring the milk and butter to the boil. Remove from the heat and tip in the flour and sugar. Whisk or beat until you have a smooth, thick paste. Then whisk in 1 egg until well mixed and then the second egg. When the pears are ready, spoon the batter over them and return to the oven for 30–35 minutes until well risen and rich brown. Serve at once with cream.

Lemon Pudding Delicious

This pudding deserves its name. Its taste and texture are magical. "As good as anything you could have", my grandmother noted down beside the recipe which I found in her kitchen notebook. I remember vividly from my childhood visits to her the melting consistency of the softly-set top and the sharp lemon flavour of the custard beneath.

2 oz butter (50 g)
8 oz castor sugar (225 g)
grated rind and juice of 2 small
lemons
4 eggs – separated
2 oz self-raising flour (50 g)
8 fl oz milk (225 ml)
½ teaspoonful cream of tartar

Butter a 2½–3-pint (1½–1¾-litre) soufflé dish. Put a roasting pan half full of water in the centre of the oven and turn on the oven to Gas Mark 4/350°F. Cream the butter until soft, add the sugar and beat until fluffy. Beat in the lemon juice and rind. Separate the yolks from the whites of the eggs and beat the yolks into the mixture. Sift the flour and stir in. Gradually stir in the milk. Beat or whisk the mixture thoroughly until very smooth. Add the cream of tartar to the egg whites and whisk until they stand in peaks. Fold gently into the pudding mixture with a metal spoon. Pour into the soufflé dish, put the dish in the pan of water and bake for 40 minutes. Serve hot or cold with or without cream.

Dum's Chocolate Pudding

Featherlight in texture with a gooey base, rich but not sickly, and just as good hot or cold – for chocolate addicts this is a winner.

5 oz plain chocolate (150 g)
5 oz margarine (150 g)
1 teaspoonful vanilla, brandy or
rum essence
¼ pint warm water (150 ml)
4 oz castor sugar (110 g)
4 eggs – separated
1 oz self-raising flour (25 g)
½ teaspoonful cream of tartar

Grease a 2½–3-pint (1½–1¾-litre) round ovenproof dish. Heat oven to Gas Mark 6/400°F and put a roasting pan half full of water on the centre shelf. Melt the chocolate with the essence and the margarine in a bowl over a pan of very hot water or in the top of a double saucepan. Add the warm water and then the sugar and stir until smooth. Pour the chocolate mixture into a mixing bowl. Stir in the egg yolks (putting the whites in a separate bowl) and then stir in the flour and beat or whisk until smooth and free of any lumps. Add the cream of tartar to the egg whites and whisk until they stand in peaks. Fold lightly into the chocolate mixture with a metal spoon. Pour into the prepared dish, put the dish into the roasting pan of water and cook at Gas Mark 6/400°F for 10 minutes and then at Gas Mark 3/325°F for 30 minutes more. Serve hot or cold with cream. If serving cold, you could whip the cream and put it on top of the pudding, and then grate some more chocolate on top of the cream.

Orange and Treacle Upside Down Pudding

A moist and spongy pudding for winter days.

2 rounded teaspoonfuls black
treacle or golden syrup
2 small oranges
2 tablespoonfuls demerara sugar
4 oz butter or margarine (110 g)
4 oz castor sugar (110 g)
2 eggs – lightly whisked
6 oz self-raising flour (175 g)
1 teaspoonful baking powder
½ teaspoonful ground cloves or
ground ginger
about ¼ pint milk (150 ml)

Heat the oven to Gas Mark 4/350°F. Butter a 7 in (18 cm) round cake tin or ovenproof dish. Spread the treacle on the bottom. Peel the oranges and cut into round, thin slices, removing any pith, and then cutting off the white pith round the edges. Arrange the orange slices over the treacle. Sprinkle the demerara sugar over them. Cream the butter and sugar in a bowl until light and fluffy. Beat in the eggs gradually and thoroughly. Sift the flour, baking powder and the ground cloves into the bowl and stir in lightly with a metal spoon, adding enough milk to give a soft dropping consistency. Spoon over the oranges and bake in the centre of the oven for just over 1 hour. Turn out on to a large plate and serve hot with cream.

19

Banana Pudding with Chocolate Sauce

This pudding is moist and light, a good way to use up squashy bananas and extremely popular with children. If you have no blender you can use a sieve or a Mouli.

about 1¾ lb bananas (810 g)
juice of ½ lemon
3 tablespoonfuls single cream or
top of the milk
3 oz castor sugar (75 g)
3 eggs – separated
1 oz self-raising flour – sifted (25 g)
½ teaspoonful cream of tartar

FOR THE SAUCE
2 oz plain chocolate (50 g)
½ oz soft brown sugar (10 g)
¼ pint milk (150 ml)

Grease a 2–2½-pint (1–1½-litre) ovenproof dish. Heat the oven to Gas Mark 4/350°F. Peel the bananas and squash them down into a blender with the lemon juice, cream, castor sugar and egg yolks. Whizz up until smooth. Add the sifted flour and whizz again. Pour into a mixing bowl. Whisk the egg whites with the cream of tartar until thick. Fold lightly into the banana mixture with a metal spoon. Pour into the greased dish and bake in the centre of the oven for 40 minutes.

About 20 minutes before the pudding is ready, make the sauce. In a pan melt the chocolate with the sugar and milk and bring to the boil. Boil for a minute or two until cream. Cool slightly, and then pour over the top of the pudding just before serving. Alternatively, make the pudding beforehand and keep warm in a low oven, making the sauce a little before you want to eat it, or have it as a cold pudding with a hot sauce. Serve with cream too if you feel particularly gluttonous.

Favourite Christmas Pudding

Makes two puddings, each feeding 8-10 people.

This is my adaptation of an old recipe for a dark, moist, full-flavoured pudding. I make it every year and it seems to have just the right mature traditional flavour. Using breadcrumbs instead of flour gives it a lighter texture.

½ teaspoonful salt
1 teaspoonful mixed spice
1 teaspoonful cinnamon
1 teaspoonful ground mace
½ teaspoonful ground cloves
8 oz shredded suet (225 g)
14 oz fresh white breadcrumbs (400 g)
grated rind and juice of 1 lemon
and 1 orange
8 oz demerara sugar (225 g)
4 oz carrots – grated (110 g)
4 oz cooking apples – grated (110 g)
12 oz raisins (350 g)
8 oz currants (225 g)
8 oz sultanas (225 g)
4 oz mixed peel (110 g)
2 oz flaked almonds (110 g)
2 tablespoonfuls black treacle
½ large wineglass of Cointreau or brandy
4 eggs, lightly whisked

Mix all the dry ingredients together thoroughly in a large bowl, including the orange and lemon rind. Melt the treacle in a pan to make it a little runny. Stir into it the lemon and orange juice, the Cointreau or brandy and finally the lightly whisked eggs. Pour the liquid into the pudding mixture and stir thoroughly. Cover the bowl with a cloth and leave until the next day. Butter two 2-pint (1-litre) basins and spoon in the pudding mixture. Cover with a double layer of buttered greaseproof paper and then either a cloth tied round with string or foil tucked in round the rim. Steam for 5–6 hours in pans of simmering water, which should be kept two thirds up the sides of the basins. When cool re-cover the basins and store in a cool place. On Christmas Day steam for a further 2–3 hours.

Baked Jam Roly Poly

Baking is quicker than steaming and makes a golden sugar crust on this homely pudding which children love.

6 oz self-raising flour (175 g)
1 rounded teaspoonful baking
powder
½ teaspoonful salt
2 oz fresh white breadcrumbs (50 g)
6 oz suet (175 g)
cold water
3–4 tablespoonfuls jam

Pre-heat the oven to Gas Mark 6/400°F. Sieve the flour, salt, baking powder together into a bowl, add the breadcrumbs and the suet and mix together. Add enough cold water (about ½ pint, 150 ml) to mix to a soft but not sticky dough. Roll out about ¼ in (½ cm) thick in a rectangle about 10 × 8 in (25½ × 20 cm). Spread evenly with jam (my children like strawberry jam best but black cherry for a special treat), leaving a border of about ½ in (1 cm) all round. Fold the border over the jam and brush with water. Roll up, starting from the shorter side. Press the top edge down lightly and press the ends together to seal. Put the roll upside down in a greased loaf tin. Cut four small slits in the top of the roll to allow steam to escape. Brush with milk and sprinkle with a little granulated sugar. Bake in the centre of the oven for 40–45 minutes until golden. Turn out on to a serving plate and serve hot with cream or custard.

Rugola

This is a Russian version of a jam roly poly in which curd cheese is incorporated in the rich pastry. Try to use good, strong-tasting jam.

8 oz self-raising flour (225 g)
1 teaspoonful baking powder
6 oz butter or margarine – at room
temperature (175 g)
6 oz fresh curd cheese (175 g)
apricot jam
3 oz raisins (75 g)
2 oz chopped almonds or hazelnuts (25 g)
a spot of milk
a sprinkling of castor sugar

Sift the flour and baking powder together into a bowl. Cut the butter and the cheese into the flour and then rub with your fingers until the ingredients blend together to form a dough. Gather into a ball, wrap up in foil and refrigerate for at least an hour or until the next day.

Heat the oven to Gas Mark 6/400°F. Knead the pastry slightly and roll out on to a floured surface into a large rectangle of about 10 × 12 in (25½ × 30 cm) and ⅛ in(3 mm) thickness. Spread fairly thickly with jam all over within ½ in (1 cm) of the edge. Sprinkle over the raisins and nuts, fold the edges in over the filling and brush with water. Then roll up fairly loosely, starting from the short end. Put into a buttered loaf tin. Brush the top of the roll with milk and sprinkle over some castor sugar. Bake in the centre of the oven for 20–25 minutes, until golden brown. Turn out and serve hot with cream.

Apricots with Walnut Cream

I love the sharp, strong taste of dried apricots. Here is a variation of stewed apricots, chilled and served with a luscious topping of cream and nuts.

8 oz dried apricots (225 g)
1 pint water (570 ml)
3 oz soft brown sugar (75 g)
juice of 1 lemon
1 oz cornflour (25 g)
¼ pint double or whipping
cream (150 g)
3 oz walnuts – chopped (75 g)
1 oz demerara sugar (25 g)

Soak the apricots in the water for at least 2 hours. Then put both the apricots and water into a pan with the brown sugar and add the lemon juice. Bring to the boil, cover and simmer gently for ¾–1 hour, until soft and mushy. Blend the cornflour with a little water to a smooth paste and then stir into the apricots. Bubble for another 3 minutes. Remove from the heat and pour into a serving dish. Cool and chill in the fridge. Then whisk the cream until thick but not stiff, stir in the chopped walnuts and spoon the mixture on top of the apricots. Sprinkle the demerara sugar on top and chill again before serving. The sugar will moisten slightly and dribble enticingly into the cream.

Dried Fruit Salad with Ginger

An excellent fruit salad for mid-winter, with the most aromatic juices.

2 × 8 oz packets of dried mixed
fruit (2 × 225 g)
2 oz crystallised ginger – cut into
small thin pieces (50 g)
4 oz demerara or granulated sugar (110 g)
juice of 2 lemons and 1 orange
2–3 tablespoonfuls dark rum

Soak the dried fruit in water overnight or for at least 6 hours. Drain it and put it into a large saucepan with the ginger, sugar and fruit juice. Bring to the boil, then cover and simmer gently for 30 minutes. Stir in the rum, transfer to a serving bowl and allow to cool. Serve with cream.

Plums in Red Wine Syrup

This is a good way to serve those plums which are sold for eating, not stewing, but which, however, are not sweet and juicy enough to be eaten on their own.

1½ lb eating plums (700 g)
8 oz granulated sugar (225 g)
¼ pint red wine (150 ml)
juice of 2 oranges and 1 lemon

Cut the plums in half, take out the stones and put into a bowl. Put the sugar in a pan with the wine and juices and dissolve over a low heat. Bring to the boil and bubble fiercely, without stirring, for 8–10 minutes or until the juice has become thicker and syrupy. Then pour the hot syrup on to the plums and stir around. Cover and leave for several hours, stirring the plums in the syrup once or twice. Serve with cream.

Stewed Pears in Fruity Syrup

Every year two old pear trees in my garden produce a lot of rock-hard pears which only the wasps seem to like. However, cooked in the oven and served in a rich syrup with cream, they are quite transformed.

2 lb hard pears (900 g)
1 heaped tablespoonful soft brown sugar
juice of 1 orange and 1 lemon
just over ¼ pint medium sweet cider (150 ml)

Peel, core and slice the pears into quarters or sixths. Arrange them in an ovenproof dish and add the sugar, the fruit juices and the cider. Cover the dish and cook in the oven at Gas Mark 3–4/325–350°F for 1½–2 hours, or until the pears are soft. Then drain the juices from the pears and chill the pears in the fridge. Boil the juices up fiercely for about 5 minutes, until they reduce a bit and thicken. Allow to cool and pour over the pears just before serving. Serve with cream.

BOP—2 **

Black Cherry Jelly

This decorative jelly is both simple to make and good to eat.

1 lb tin black cherries (450 g)
1 oz blanched almonds (25 g)
grated rind and juice of 2 lemons
½ oz or 1 packet gelatine (10 g)

hot water
¼ pint double or whipping cream
(150 ml)
1 oz plain chocolate (25 g)

Drain the juice from the cherries. Put the cherries in the bottom of a 2-pint (1-litre) round dish with the blanched almonds. Grate the lemon rind and put on one side. Strain the lemon juice into the cherry juice and add 6 tablespoonfuls of hot water. Dissolve the gelatine in 3 tablespoons of hot water and stir into the warm cherry liquid. Pour over the cherries and leave until set. Chill in the fridge. Then dip the dish briefly in hot water and turn the jelly out on to a serving plate. Whisk the cream until stiff, stir in the lemon rind and pile evenly on top of the jelly. Coarsely grate the chocolate on top. Chill again in the fridge before serving.

Syrup Pikelets

Children love these light little pancakes. They can be eaten simply buttered for tea, or served with a fruit purée, or you can make two to three large pancakes out of the mixture, spread them with jam or honey and then roll them up and serve with cream.

4 oz plain flour (110 g)
1 oz castor sugar (25 g)
1 egg – lightly whisked
juice of ½ lemon

approximately 6 fl oz milk (175 ml)
2 rounded teaspoonfuls
baking powder
golden syrup

Sift the flour and sugar together into a bowl. Stir in the egg, the lemon juice and about 6 fl oz of milk and beat with a wooden spoon or whisk until smooth. Then beat or whisk in the baking powder. Heat an ungreased hot plate or a large, heavy pan to a medium heat and drop on tablespoonfuls of the mixture, allowing room for them to spread. When the spoonfuls bubble, turn with a spatula and cook on the other side. Put on a hot serving dish and pour over some warmed golden syrup.

Baked Pancakes with Orange Sauce

These are like light, sweet Yorkshire puddings so they have to be served at once. Mix the sauce and keep it warm in the oven. Have the batter ready in patty tins to pop into the oven just as everyone is starting the first course.

FOR THE SAUCE
2 tablespoonfuls golden syrup
2 oz butter (50 g)
grated rind and juice of 1 orange
juice of $\frac{1}{2}$ lemon

FOR THE PANCAKES
2 oz margarine (50 g)
2 oz castor sugar (50 g)
2 eggs
2 oz self-raising flour (50 g)
pinch of salt
1 teaspoonful lemon juice
8 fl oz milk (225 ml)

Make the sauce first by warming the ingredients together and stirring together until blended. Keep it warm in a low oven or in a double boiler. Then cream the margarine and sugar together until light and fluffy. Beat in the eggs thoroughly, one at a time. Sift in the flour and salt and lightly stir in the lemon juice. Stir in the milk and beat to a smooth, thin batter (If the mixture should curdle, whizz it up in a liquidiser for a moment or two.) Heat the oven to Gas Mark 7/425°F. (Move the sauce to the top of the stove if it is in the oven.) Grease some patty tins. The mixture will fill 16–18 tins, so you may have to have one lot of tins or little dishes below the others, cooking them for a little longer. Pour the mixture up to almost the top of the tins and bake at the top of the oven for 15–20 minutes, until well risen. Serve at once with the warmed sauce and cream if liked.

Toffee Crunch Delight

A perfect family pudding, which is easy to make. Children love the bits of golden toffee and adults equally enjoy the creamy nutty rice and the tang of orange.

1 cup pudding rice
2½ cups water
6 oz granulated sugar (175 g)
3 tablespoonfuls water
pinch of cream of tartar
8 fl oz double or whipping cream
(225 ml)
2 round tablespoonfuls castor sugar
4 oz cottage cheese (110 g)
grated rind of 1 large orange
¼–½ a whole nutmeg – grated

Bring the water to the boil, add the rice and simmer for about 10 minutes until it is just tender – it should still have a slight bite to it. Drain in a large sieve and rinse thoroughly with cold water. Leave to cool completely. Meanwhile make the toffee. Put the granulated sugar, 3 tablespoonfuls of water and the cream of tartar into a pan. Bring to the boil, stirring until the sugar is dissolved. Then boil without stirring for 3 – 5 minutes, until a blob sets hard on a plate or the temperature reaches the crack mark on a sugar thermometer. Pour the toffee thinly on to an oiled tray and leave on one side.

When the rice is cold, whip the cream until fairly thick, whisk in the castor sugar and then stir in the cottage cheese, the orange rind and the grated nutmeg. Keep this mixture in the fridge until needed. Shortly before your meal, break the toffee up into small pieces. Stir just over half of it into the rice mixture, transfer to a serving bowl and sprinkle the remaining toffee on top.

Spiced Seville Rice

(serves 4 or 5)

A very quickly made cold rice pudding. If you want to make it more sophisticated, mix the marmalade with dark rum instead of lemon juice.

grated rind and juice of 1 large
orange
1 pint warm milk (570 ml)
2 oz ground rice (50 g)
2 level teaspoonfuls ground
allspice or nutmeg

2 oz soft dark brown sugar (50 g)
1 carton soured cream
3 tablespoonfuls orange jelly
marmalade
juice of 1 lemon

Grate the orange rind into a pan of warm milk. Add the ground rice and the spice. Bring to the boil, stirring continuously. Simmer for 3 minutes. Add the brown sugar. Take off the heat and gradually stir in the orange juice and then the soured cream. Put into individual serving dishes or glasses. Gently melt the jelly marmalade in a pan with the lemon juice. Spoon this syrup over the puddings and chill in the fridge before serving.

Spanish Creams

Children run to four helpings of this light mousse. Perhaps it is the small amount of sherry in it which gives them a kick!

1 level tablespoonful arrowroot
1 pint milk (570 ml)
2 eggs – separated
2 tablespoonfuls single cream
2 oz castor sugar (50 g)

grated rind of 1 orange
2 tablespoonfuls sweet sherry
2 oz sweet almonds – chopped (50 g)

Blend the arrowroot until smooth with 2 tablespoonfuls of the milk. Add to the rest of the milk in a saucepan and bring to the boil. Boil for 1 minute. Allow to cool until not unbearably hot. Mix the egg yolks, cream, sugar and orange rind thoroughly in a mixing bowl. Gradually stir in the hot, thickened milk and then the sherry. Leave until cold. Then whisk the egg whites until stiff and fold into the milk mixture. Transfer to small individual dishes or to a serving bowl and sprinkle the top with the chopped nuts. Chill in the fridge before serving, but eat the same day.

OLD-FASHIONED PUDDINGS

Mint and Currant Tart

This is an adaptation of an old Yorkshire recipe and is a good and unusual combination of flavours. The sweet pastry holds its shape very well and yet remains rich and tender.

FOR THE PASTRY
8 oz strong plain flour (225 g)
2 tablespoonfuls icing sugar
4 oz butter or margarine (110 g)
2 oz lard (50 g)

FOR THE FILLING
a handful of fresh mint
leaves – finely chopped
8 oz currants (225 g)
1 rounded tablespoonful castor sugar

Make the pastry beforehand. Sift the flour and icing sugar into a bowl. Cut in the butter and lard and crumble with your fingertips until the mixture is like coarse breadcrumbs. Using a knife, stir in a very little very cold water until the mixture only just begins to stick together. Then press into a ball, wrap in cling film or foil and chill in the fridge for at least 1 hour.

Heat the oven to Gas Mark 6/400°F. Then in a bowl mix the chopped mint with the currants and castor sugar. Cut the pastry in half and form into two balls. Butter a shallow 8–8½ in (20–21 cm) flan dish, preferably the fluted metal kind, with a push-up base. Roll out one half of the pastry on a floured surface into a circle big enough to line the flan dish. Line it and press the rolling pin over the edges to cut the overlapping pastry off neatly. Prick the bottom lightly with a fork and spoon in the currant mixture.

Add the pastry trimmings to the other half of the pastry and roll out into a circle big enough for the top. Moisten the bottom edges and lay the second circle of pastry on top. Again press the rolling pin over the edges to cut off the surplus pastry. Prick all over with a fork and, if you like, roll out the trimmings to cut out decorations for the tart (mint leaves and currants would be appropriate). Brush the tart with a little milk and bake in the centre of the oven for 25–30 minutes until light golden brown. If cooked in a loose-bottomed flan tin turn the tart out on to a serving dish. Serve warm with cream. For an extra treat stir a little brandy into the cream.

Old-Fashioned Carrot Tart

Carrots contain the same kind of sugar as the juice of the sugar cane and have a perfect flavour, colour and texture for puddings. But the habit of using them for puddings is long past and nowadays people are amazed when you produce something like this brilliant orange glossy tart. Don't be put off by the list of ingredients – it's straightforward to make.

FOR THE PASTRY
5 oz plain flour (150 g)
½ teaspoonful salt
2 oz icing sugar (50 g)
3 oz butter or margarine – at room temperature (75 g)
1 egg – whisked lightly

FOR THE FILLING
2 oz butter (50 g)
2 eggs
1 yolk

8 fl oz single cream (225 ml)
4 oz castor sugar (110 g)
2 oz fresh white breadcrumbs (50 g)
grated rind of 1 lemon
3 oz grated carrot (75 g)
½ a whole nutmeg – grated

FOR THE TOPPING
8 oz carrots (225 g)
8 oz granulated sugar (225 g)
juice of 1 lemon
4 tablespoonfuls water

Make the pastry in advance. Sift the flour, salt and icing sugar into a mixing bowl. Make a well in the centre and drop in the egg and the butter. Work together with your hands until well blended – if the butter is really soft this will only take a minute. Then knead lightly with the palms of your hands (flour them to stop them being sticky), until you have a smooth ball of dough. Leave in the fridge for at least half an hour.

To make the filling melt the butter and leave to cool slightly. In a mixing bowl whisk together the eggs, the melted butter, the cream and the sugar. Stir in the bread-crumbs, lemon rind, the grated carrot and the grated nutmeg. Heat the oven to Gas Mark 4/350°F and butter a 10–10½ in (25.5–26.5 cm) flan dish (preferably with a removable base as the crisp sweet pastry turns out perfectly). Roll the pastry out on to a well-floured board in a circle a little bigger than the flan dish. Line the flan dish with the pastry, turning the slightly overlapping edges in again to make a thicker, neat edge. Prick the base all over with a fork. Pour in the prepared filling and bake in the centre of the oven for 45–50 minutes until golden and slightly risen.

To prepare the topping, cut the carrots in thin slices and chop into little pieces. Put them in a saucepan with the sugar, lemon juice and water and boil for 5–10 minutes until a blob of the syrup sets on a cold saucer. Allow to cool a little before spreading all over the top of the tart. Serve the tart cold but not chilled, with or without cream.

Orange Pudding in Tangy Sauce

This is a light steamed pudding which looks lovely as it plops out and the sharp sweet syrup runs down on to the serving plate.

grated rind and juice of 1 large
lemon and 1 orange
4 oz demerara sugar (110 g)
3 eggs – separated
5 oz castor sugar (150 g)
juice of 1 extra orange
scant 1 oz self-raising flour (25 g)
scant 1 oz cornflour (25 g)
$\frac{1}{2}$ teaspoonful salt

Have ready a 2-pint (1-litre) soufflé dish. Grate the rinds of the lemon and 1 orange and put on one side. Squeeze out the juice and strain into a saucepan. Add the demerara sugar and dissolve in the juices over a low heat. Then boil fiercely without stirring for 2–3 minutes until the syrup is reduced and thickened. Pour the syrup into the soufflé dish and run it all round the edges, spreading it round with a knife as it cools if necessary, until the syrup coats both the sides and bottom of the dish. Beat the egg yolks and castor sugar until pale. Gradually beat in the juice of the second orange and the reserved lemon and orange rind. Sift the flour and cornflour on to the mixture and stir in. Whisk the egg whites with the salt until stiff and fold into the yolk and orange mixture with a metal spoon. Pour into the prepared soufflé dish and put into a large saucepan with water coming halfway up the dish. Cover the pan and put over a low heat so the water barely simmers for 1–1½ hours, until firm to touch in the centre. Turn out on to a serving plate and serve hot with cream. If the pudding is cooked but you are not ready to eat it, simply turn off the heat and leave the dish sitting in the hot water in the covered saucepan until ready to serve.

Apricot and Honey Spice Pudding

A specially tasty and light-textured steamed pudding, perfect for winter family lunches.

6 oz self-raising flour (175 g)
1 level teaspoonful baking powder
1 teaspoonful salt
1 level teaspoonful cinnamon
½ teaspoonful ground cloves
3 oz fresh white breadcrumbs (75 g)
4 oz shredded suet (110 g)
6 oz dried apricots, chopped – or
cranberries in season (175 g)
6 fl oz milk (175)
1 egg
4 tablespoonfuls honey – melted

Sift the flour, baking powder, salt and spices into a mixing bowl. Stir in the breadcrumbs, suet and chopped apricots. Whisk the egg with the milk and stir in. Then thoroughly stir in the melted honey. Grease a 2-pint (1-litre) pudding basin and put the mixture in. Cover with a piece of foil folded in a pleat to allow the pudding to expand as it cooks. Tie the foil on tightly with string. It's useful for taking the pudding out if you make a string handle as well. Place the pudding in a large saucepan and fill with boiling water to come about halfway up the side of the basin. Cover the pan with a tightly fitting lid and simmer gently for 2½–3 hours. Check once or twice to see if the boiling water needs topping up. Turn out and serve with cream.

Sussex Pond Pudding

Everyone breaks their diet for this famous steamed pudding. Eating it is like an orgy as it could hardly be more fattening or more delicious! A golden brown and flaky suet crust encases the lemon butter juices which seep out when you turn the pudding out thus forming the "pond". You can give each person a slice of the whole soft, sharp lemon. The maximum boiling time is best so remember to prepare well ahead.

6 oz self-raising flour (175 g)
1 level teaspoonful baking powder
½ teaspoonful salt
2 oz fresh white breadcrumbs (50 g)
4 oz suet (110 g)
¼ pint or a little more mixed cold milk and water (150 ml)
6 oz butter (175 g)
6 oz demerara sugar (175 g)
1 large lemon

Sift the flour, salt and baking powder into a mixing bowl. Stir in the breadcrumbs and suet. With a round-bladed knife mix in the milk and the water until you have a soft, elastic dough. Form the dough into a ball on a floured board. Generously butter a 2-pint (1-litre) pudding basin. Cut off a quarter of the dough and set aside for the lid. Roll out the large piece of dough into a circle about 2 in (5 cm) wider than the top of the pudding basin and line the basin with this pastry, pressing it to shape.

Cut the butter into rough pieces and put half of it with half the sugar into the pastry-lined basin. Prick the lemon all over with a skewer and lay it on the butter and sugar. Then put the remaining butter and sugar on top. If the mixture is far below the top of the basin you can add some more butter and sugar. Fold the edges of the pastry in over the filling and moisten. Roll out the remaining pastry into a circle to form the lid and lay it on top, pressing the edges to seal. Butter a piece of foil, make a pleat in the middle and put it over the basin. Tie down with string and make a string handle for lifting out the pudding. Put enough water into a large saucepan to come halfway up the pudding basin. Bring the water to the boil and then lower the pudding into it. Cover and simmer for 3–4 hours, topping up with boiling water if necessary. Turn the pudding out on to a serving dish large enough for the juices to seep out round it. Serve hot with cream.

The Duke of Northumberland's Pudding

This is an adaptation of a recipe written in 1790. It's a buttery steamed pudding to hearten cold winter days. It has a delicious brandy flavour, rises well and is best served as the Duke would have had it, with brandy butter. But of course you can use cream or custard instead.

4 oz sultanas (110 g)
2–3 tablespoonfuls brandy
4 oz fresh breadcrumbs (110 g)
2 oz suet (50 g)
2 oz soft brown sugar (50 g)
$\frac{1}{2}$ teaspoonful salt
$\frac{1}{4}$ of a whole nutmeg
grated rind of 1 lemon
2 oz butter – melted (50 g)
3 eggs – whisked
$\frac{1}{2}$ teaspoonful bicarbonate of soda

Soak the sultanas in the brandy in a covered mixing bowl for 1–2 hours. Then mix in the breadcrumbs, suet, sugar, salt, nutmeg and lemon rind. Stir in the melted butter and the eggs. Dissolve the bicarbonate of soda in a little cold water and mix in. Generously butter a 2-pint (1-litre) pudding basin and put the mixture in. Cover with a piece of buttered foil, tie down with string and make a string handle for lifting the pudding out. Lower into a pan of boiling water which should come halfway up the sides of the basin. Cover and simmer for 2–2$\frac{1}{2}$ hours, topping up with boiling water if necessary. Turn out on to a serving dish.

Guards' Pudding

Everyone in our house votes this their favourite hot pudding. It is a steamed pudding which is light, buttery, strawberry flavoured and not at all stodgy.

5 oz fresh brown or white
breadcrumbs (150 g)
1 oz self-raising flour (25 g)
4 oz castor sugar (110 g)
5 rounded tablespoonfuls
strawberry jam – melted
3 eggs – whisked
4 oz butter or margarine – melted
(110 g)
1 level teaspoonful bicarbonate of soda

Grease well a 2–2½-pint (1–1.25-litre) pudding basin. Into a mixing bowl put the breadcrumbs, the flour and the sugar. Stir in the melted jam, the whisked eggs and the melted butter. Dissolve the bicarbonate of soda in a very little cold water and stir thoroughly into the mixture. Pour into the prepared basin. Cover with a double layer of greased foil or greaseproof paper, pleated in the middle to allow the pudding to rise. Tie the foil tightly down with string and make a string handle. Put into a large saucepan with enough boiling water to come halfway up the basin. Cover with a lid and simmer for 2 hours, checking occasionally to see if the water needs topping up. Turn out and serve with cream.

Lemon and Honey Pudding

My family always gorge themselves with this golden yellow, open-textured, steamed pudding. It is oozing with honey and perfect to cheer a wintry day.

2 rounded tablespoonfuls honey
2 oz self-raising flour (50 g)
1 teaspoonful baking powder
$\frac{1}{2}$ teaspoonful salt
4 oz fresh white breadcrumbs (110 g)
6 oz suet (175 g)
4 oz castor sugar (110 g)
3 eggs
3 heaped tablespoonfuls lemon curd
grated rind and juice of 1 lemon

Butter a 2-pint (1-litre) pudding basin and spoon the honey into the bottom. Sift the flour, baking powder and salt together into a mixing bowl. Add the bread-crumbs, suet and sugar and stir well together. In a small bowl beat the eggs and the lemon curd lightly together with a fork and stir into the pudding mixture. Lastly, stir in the lemon rind and juice. Pour the mixture into the prepared pudding basin and cover with a double layer of buttered greaseproof paper or foil, pleated in the middle to allow the pudding to rise. Tie the paper securely down with string and make a string handle. Put the pudding into a large saucepan with enough boiling water to come halfway up the sides of the basin. Cover tightly and simmer gently for 2–2$\frac{1}{2}$ hours. Check once or twice to see if the water needs topping up. Turn out and serve hot with cream.

Queen of Puddings

Queen Charlotte considered this pudding most nutritious and encouraged the patients in her hospital to eat it. It has become the most famous and certainly the favourite nursery pudding, not only for children but for adults too.

3 oz fresh white breadcrumbs (75 g)
grated rind of 1 lemon
½ pint single cream (275 ml)
½ pint milk (275 ml) } **or 1 pint milk (570 ml)**
2 oz butter or margarine (50 g)
3 eggs – separated
5 oz castor sugar (150 g)
about 4 rounded tablespoonfuls
strawberry jam

Heat oven to Gas Mark 4/350°F. Butter a baking dish. Put the breadcrumbs into the dish. Grate the lemon rind into the milk and cream in a saucepan with the butter and heat until just warm. Beat the egg yolks lightly together with 3 oz (75 g) of the sugar in a mixing bowl. Gradually stir the heated milk into them. Pour this mixture over the breadcrumbs and bake in the centre of the oven for about 25 minutes or until set. Remove from the oven and spread the jam over the top. Whisk the egg whites until stiff and fold in the remaining sugar. Pile this meringue over the jam and return to the oven for another 15 minutes until golden and crisp. Serve hot or cold, with or without cream.

General Satisfaction

This Victorian nursery pudding, with its charmingly modest but apt name, is in character with Queen of Puddings, and is one of so many puddings with soft meringue tops which fill the pages of late nineteenth-century cookery books.

2 teaspoonfuls cornflour
¾ pint milk (425 ml)
3 large eggs
2 tablespoonfuls castor sugar
½ teaspoonful vanilla essence
3–4 tablespoonfuls apricot jam
12–14 sponge fingers
1 tablespoonful plus 2
teaspoonfuls sherry (optional)
3 oz castor sugar (75 g)

Blend the cornflour with a tablespoonful of the milk and add to the rest of the milk in a saucepan. Bring to the boil, stirring, and bubble for 2 minutes. Remove from the heat. Lightly whisk 1 whole egg and 2 yolks (putting the remaining whites into a bowl) and stir into the hot milk. Then stir over a low heat, keeping just below boiling until the custard thickens enough to coat the back of the spoon. This should only take 1–2 minutes. Add 2 tablespoonfuls castor sugar and ½ teaspoonful vanilla essence. Cool. Heat the oven to Gas Mark 4/350°F. Spread the jam over the bottom of a fairly shallow ovenproof dish. Lay the sponge fingers over the jam and sprinkle with a tablespoonful of sherry. Unless it is very smooth, strain the cooled custard through a sieve over the sponge fingers. Whisk the egg whites until stiff. Then add all but a little of the sugar and 2 teaspoonfuls of sherry and whisk again thoroughly. Spread the meringue over the custard and sprinkle on the remaining sugar. Put the dish in the centre of the oven for 10–15 minutes until pale brown. Serve cold with or without cream.

Orange and Ginger Baked Custard

Baked custard is simple to make and I love it. This is an interesting variation.

juice of 4 large oranges and grated
rind of 1
2 oz castor sugar (50 g)
1 level teaspoonful ground ginger
¼ pint single cream (150 ml)
3 eggs

Grate the rind of 1 orange and put on one side. Squeeze the juice out of the oranges and strain it into a bowl. Stir in the sugar, ground ginger and the cream. Whisk the eggs lightly and strain into the mixture. Stir again. Heat the oven to Gas Mark 3/325°F. Have a shallow pan of water ready just below the centre of the oven. Pour the custard mixture into an ovenproof dish and put the dish in the pan of water. Bake for 45–60 minutes until set. Cool and decorate the top of the custard with the grated orange rind. Serve cold with thin sweet biscuits.

Iceberg Pudding

To me this old-fashioned pudding is archetypal English nursery fare. I believe that its true name is Snow Pudding but my children think that the frothy white mould looks much more like an iceberg floating in a sea of vanilla custard. It has a delicate lemon flavour and slips irresistibly down the throat.

2 lemons
1 pint water (570 ml)
4 oz sugar (110 g)
2½ tablespoonfuls cornflour
3 large eggs
¾ pint milk (425 ml)
1 oz castor sugar (25 g)
½ teaspoonful vanilla essence

Grate the rind of the lemons and keep on one side. Put the water and sugar on to boil. Mix the cornflour until smooth with the juice of the lemons and another tablespoonful of water. Stir this mixture into the pan of water and add the lemon rind. Bubble gently for 2–3 minutes until thickened. Meanwhile put the egg yolks aside in a bowl and whisk the whites until stiff. Take the thickened mixture off the heat and add the whisked egg whites, whisking them thoroughly into the mixture. Pour into a 2-pint (1-litre) mould or pudding basin and leave to cool. When cool chill well in the fridge. Meanwhile make the custard. Bring the milk, sugar and essence to boiling point. Remove from the heat and pour gradually on to the egg yolks, stirring with a wooden spoon. Strain the mixture through a sieve back into the saucepan or, preferably, into the top of a double saucepan. Cook over a very low heat – it must not boil – stirring all the time until the custard thickens enough to thinly coat the back of the spoon, about 4–8 minutes. Leave to get cold. When the pudding is chilled turn it out on to a large serving dish and pour the custard all round, but not over it.

Fraises à l'Orange

The combination of strawberries and orange juice is specially good in this old French recipe.

1½ lb strawberries (700 g)
castor sugar
juice of 2 oranges

Remove the stalks from the strawberries. Put aside 1 lb (450 g) of the best ones. Put the other ½ lb (250 g) through a fine sieve and mix the purée thoroughly with a tablespoonful of castor sugar and the orange juice. Put the purée into a shallow serving dish and arrange the whole strawberries over it. Sprinkle with castor sugar and chill well in the fridge before serving.

Lemon Honeycomb Mould

Jane Grigson revived this excellent nursery pudding in her lovely book, Good Things. *It certainly is delicious – a fresh three-layered jelly of contrasting consistencies. Well worth making for any occasion.*

3 eggs – separated
the roughly grated rind and juice of
2 lemons
3 oz castor sugar (75 g)
½ oz or 1 packet gelatine (10 g)
6 tablespoonfuls cream
¾ pint milk – Gold Top if possible
(425 ml)

Put the egg yolks in a large bowl. Add the lemon rind (but not the juice), sugar, gelatine and cream and stir together. Heat the milk until just under boiling point and whisk thoroughly into the yolk mixture. Set the bowl over a large pan of simmering water and stir with a wooden spoon until slightly thickened (about the consistency of cream). Remove the bowl from the heat and gradually stir in the lemon juice. Whisk the egg whites until stiff, then strain the lemon custard on to them and fold in with a metal spoon. Pour into a 2-pint (1-litre) jelly mould. Cool and chill in the fridge. Sometimes the jelly will turn out of the mould with a good shake – if it doesn't, dip the mould in very hot water for just a moment and then turn out on to a serving plate.

Chocolate Layer Pudding

This is an old chocolate pudding recipe from a country house cook's notebook in the North of England. It is made very easily with layers of thin bread and chocolate, topped with cream and chilled in the fridge. It is rich and delicious, equally suitable for a dinner party or for a children's lunch, though for a party you may like to substitute a small glassful of rum or brandy for the orange juice.

8 oz plain chocolate (225 g)
¾ pint milk (425 ml)
juice of 1 large orange
about ½ lb thinly sliced white bread (225 g)
¼ pint double cream (150 ml)

Break up the chocolate (reserving one square to grate on top of the pudding) and boil it with the milk until it becomes creamy and thickened – about 5 minutes. Strain in the orange juice and stir. Cut the crusts off the thin slices of bread and cut the slices in half. Pour a thin layer of chocolate over the bottom of a 2-pint (1-litre) soufflé dish. Follow with a layer of pieces of bread, then more chocolate and more bread, ending with a layer of chocolate. Cool. When cold whip the cream until thick and put on top of the chocolate. Grate the reserved square of chocolate on top of the cream. Chill well in the fridge before serving.

PIES, TARTS AND FLANS

Apple and Raisin Fudge Pie

The inside of this pie tastes rather like Apfel Strudel and the easy flaky pastry is deliciously crisp.

FOR THE PASTRY
8 oz strong plain flour – the strong
bread flour is good for this pastry (225 g)
good pinch of salt
6 oz (175 g) from an 8 oz (225 g)
block of frozen butter or margarine
6 tablespoonfuls cold
water – preferably from the fridge
sprinkling of castor sugar

FOR THE FILLING
2 lb cooking apples (900 g)
3 oz butter or margarine (75 g)
5 oz soft brown sugar (150 g)
grated rind of 1 lemon
4 oz raisins (110 g)

First make your pastry. Sift the flour and salt into a bowl. Put a grater into the bowl on top of the flour. Hold the frozen butter in its wrapping and coarsely grate off three quarters of the block. With a palette knife quickly mix the fat in with the flour until crumbly. Now add the water, gradually mixing it with the palette knife. Then gather the dough up in your hands and press it together into a ball. Wrap in foil or plastic and leave in the fridge.

Peel and core the apples and cut in fairly small pieces. Melt the butter and sugar in a large pan. Add the apples and bubble them in the fudge syrup over the highest heat, stirring often, for 3–4 minutes. Remove from the heat and stir in the lemon rind and raisins. Put into a 9–10 in (23–25.5 cm) shallow pie dish or a flan dish and leave to cool. When completely cold turn the oven to Gas Mark 6/400°F. Roll out the pastry a little larger than the pie dish. Moisten the edges of the pie dish and lay the pastry on top. Cut off the edges and roll out the trimmings to cut out decorations. Brush with cold water, sprinkle with a little castor sugar and bake in the centre of the oven for 35–40 minutes until golden brown. Serve warm with cream.

49

Blackcurrant Pie

Sharp and refreshing blackcurrants sandwiched between rich crispy pastry and a bottom layer of bread soaked with the dark, delicious juices.

FOR THE PASTRY
8 oz plain flour (225 g)
good pinch of salt
6 oz (175 g) from an 8 oz (225 g)
block of frozen butter or margarine
6 tablespoonfuls very cold
water – preferably from the fridge

FOR THE PIE FILLING
2–3 thin slices white bread
1 lb blackcurrants (450 g)
4 oz castor sugar (110 g)

Make your pastry first. Sift the flour and salt into a bowl. Put a grater into the bowl on top of the flour. Hold the frozen butter in its wrapping and coarsely grate off three quarters of the block. Using a palette knife mix the fat roughly into the flour. Now add the water gradually, mixing again with the knife and then gather the dough up with your hands and press into a ball. Wrap in foil or plastic and leave in the fridge for at least 30 minutes. Heat the oven to Gas Mark 6/400°F.

For the filling cut the crusts off the bread and line an 8–9 in (20–23 cm) shallow pie dish or flan dish with the bread, cutting it to shape. Top and tail the blackcurrants and wash them well in a colander. Drain them and mix them in a bowl with the sugar. Spoon the mixture on top of the bread in the pie dish. Then roll out the pastry slightly larger than the pie dish, moisten the edges of the dish and lay the pastry on top. Cut off the edges neatly and roll out the trimmings to decorate the pie. Brush with cold water and sprinkle all over with castor sugar. Bake in the centre of the oven for 30–40 minutes or until rich golden brown. Serve warm with cream.

Banana and Walnut Pie

If you use packet puff pastry this rich, scrumptious pie is very simple to prepare.

8 oz packet puff pastry (225 g)
8 oz full cream cheese (225 g)
3 oz soft brown sugar (75 g)
1 egg – lightly whisked
3–4 bananas
2–3 oz walnuts – chopped (50–75 g)
spot of milk
castor sugar

Butter an 8–9 in (20–23 cm) flan dish and heat oven to Gas Mark 7/425°F. Cut the pastry in half and shape into two balls. Roll out two circles of about the size of the flan dish, one slightly larger. Prick all over with a fork and line the flan dish with the larger circle. Put the cream cheese and brown sugar into a bowl and cream together. Beat in the egg. Slice the bananas in rounds and stir them into the mixture with the chopped nuts. Spoon the mixture into the lined flan dish and put the other circle of pastry on top. Cut the edges off neatly and press down lightly. Roll out the trimmings to decorate. Brush with milk and sprinkle liberally with castor sugar. Bake in the centre of the oven for 25–35 minutes until the pastry is a rich crispy brown. Serve hot or cold with cream.

Apple and Elderberry Pie

At the end of the summer use the delicately flavoured elderberries in an apple pie instead of blackberries. As this is a double crust plate pie try this version of American pie pastry – it's made in an easy but quite different way from English shortcrust and has the lightest, most melting texture.

FOR THE PASTRY
7 oz lard or vegetable fat (200 g)
2½ tablespoonfuls water
½ teaspoonful salt
10 oz strong white flour (275 g)
sprinkling of castor sugar

FOR THE FILLING
2 lb cooking apples (900 g)
5 oz castor sugar (150 g)
1 oz butter (25 g)
a good handful of elderberries

Make the pastry beforehand. Put the lard, water and salt into a mixing bowl and beat or whisk together until light and fluffy. Sift the flour on to the softened fat and mix it in with a round bladed knife until you have a rough paste. Form into a ball with your hands, wrap in foil or plastic and chill for at least 1 hour.

While the pastry is in the fridge, peel and slice the apples and put into a pan with the sugar. Cook over a medium heat, stirring fairly often until the apples go mushy and absorb the sugar syrup. Then stir in the butter. Leave to cool. Push the elderberries off their stalks and stir them into the cooked apples.

Take the pastry from the fridge, knead lightly and cut in half. Roll out one half into a circle big enough to line an 8–9 in (20–23 cm) pie plate. (The pastry is very short so roll it carefully back over the rolling pin and gently out again on to the pie plate. If it breaks up at all push it back together again.) Spoon the apples and elderberry mixture into the lined pie plate, roll out the other half of the pastry and lay on top, pressing the edges down to seal and decorating with patterns made from the pastry trimmings. (If you have time it is always better to put pies back into the fridge for some time before baking as it makes the pastry even lighter and less likely to shrink during the cooking.) Heat the oven to Gas Mark 6/400°F. Brush the pie lightly with cold water and sprinkle with a little castor sugar. Bake in the centre of the oven for 25–35 minutes until the pastry is golden brown. Serve hot or cold with cream.

American Apricot Pie

An excellent large fruit pie for all the family with a soft, half-bread, half-cake base and a delicious crunchy top. When apricots are out of season you can use apples, pears or plums instead.

1 teaspoonful dried yeast
4 tablespoonfuls warm water
6 oz plus 1 teaspoonful castor sugar (175 g)
3 oz pure vegetable fat (75 g)
1 egg
8 oz plain flour (225 g)
1 teaspoonful baking powder
½ teaspoonful salt
5 fl oz soured cream (150 ml)
1 lb fresh apricots (450 g)

FOR THE TOPPING
2 oz butter or margarine (50 g)
4 oz soft brown sugar (110 g)
2 oz plain flour (50 g)
1 teaspoonful ground cinnamon
2 oz walnuts – chopped roughly (50 g)

Dissolve the yeast and the teaspoonful of sugar in the warm water and put on one side. Cream the fat, the 6 oz (175 g) castor sugar and the egg together until light and fluffy. Sift the flour, baking powder and salt together. Stir the soured cream into the yeast and water and add it to the creamed mixture alternately with the sifted flour, mixing well after each addition. Spread the batter into a greased 9½–10 in (24–25.5 cm) flan dish or rectangular ovenproof dish. Heat the oven to Gas Mark 4/350°F. Cut the apricots in half, remove the stones and slice fairly thinly. Arrange on top of the batter. To make the topping, simply melt the butter and stir in the other ingredients. Sprinkle the mixture over the apricots and bake in the centre of the oven for 1 hour – if the top gets too brown lay a piece of foil on it. Serve warm or cold with cream.

Cream Cheese and Mincemeat Pocket

This is a delicious mixture of mincemeat (best of all if it's homemade with brandy) and cream cheese which oozes out of a flaky pastry case with a crispy top.

1 lb packet puff pastry (450 g)
6–8 oz full cream cheese (175–225 g)
2 oz castor sugar (50 g)
½ lb mincemeat (225 g)
spot of milk
sprinkling of castor sugar

Cut the pastry in half and roll out into two rectangles approximately 6 × 8 in (15 × 20 cm) (or into a square if it's easier). Prick all over with a fork and leave to rest for about 15 minutes. Heat the oven to Gas Mark 7/425°F. Put the cream cheese and the sugar into a bowl and beat with a wooden spoon until smooth. Grease a baking sheet. Put one of the pastry pieces (if there is any difference, the one which is slightly larger) on the sheet. Spread half the cream cheese on to one pastry piece within ¾ in (2 cm) of the edges and the other half on the second piece. Moisten the edges of both. Spread the mincemeat on top of the piece on the baking sheet and carefully lift the other piece and put it on top, cream cheese side down. Press the edges together and over to make a double rim. Pinch to form a neat border. Cut two small slits in the centre. Brush with milk and sprinkle generously all over with castor sugar. Bake just above the centre of the oven for 20–25 minutes, until well risen and golden brown. Leave to cool for about 5 minutes. With the help of two wide knives or spatulas lift carefully on to a large serving plate. Best eaten lukewarm with or without cream.

Lemon Tart

A light lemony tart which is equally good, and different, hot or cold. If you have it cold during the summer arrange a layer of halved strawberries or raspberries on the top before sprinkling with the icing sugar.

FOR THE PASTRY
6 oz strong plain flour (175 g)
1 heaped tablespoonful icing sugar
3 oz butter (75 g)
2 oz lard (50 g)

FOR THE FILLING
2 oz butter (50 g)
3 oz castor sugar (75 g)
grated rind and juice of 1 lemon
2 eggs – separated
1 oz self-raising flour (25 g)
6 tablespoonfuls milk
icing sugar

Make the pastry first. Sift the flour and the icing sugar into a bowl. Cut in the fat and then crumble with your fingertips until the mixture resembles rough breadcrumbs. Add only two teaspoonfuls of very cold water and stir round with a knife until the mixture begins to cling together. Press into a ball, wrap in plastic or foil and chill for at least 30 minutes in the fridge. Heat the oven to Gas Mark 5/375°F. Grease a 9 in (23 cm) flan dish or tin, preferably one with a push-up base. Knead the pastry a little and roll out on a floured board into a circle a little larger than the flan dish. Line the dish with the pastry, pressing round the edge with a rolling pin to cut off a neat edge.

Beat the butter until soft and then beat in the castor sugar until light and fluffy. Beat in the lemon rind and juice followed by the egg yolks. Sift the flour on to the mixture and stir it in. Gradually stir in the milk. Whisk the egg whites until they stand in soft peaks and, using a metal spoon, fold them gently but thoroughly into the yolk mixture. Pour into the flan dish and cook in the centre of the oven for 25–30 minutes until firm to a soft touch in the centre. Serve hot or cold with cream. Just before serving sprinkle with a little icing sugar through a sieve. If it is to be eaten cold, keep in a cool place but not the fridge.

Tangy Treacle Tart

In this delicious version of the famous English dish the lemon juice and rind counteracts the sweetness of the syrup and the rich pastry melts in your mouth.

FOR THE PASTRY
8 oz plain flour (225 g)
$\frac{1}{2}$ teaspoonful salt
4 oz butter or margarine (110 g)
2 oz lard (50 g)
1 egg yolk
grated rind and juice of 1 lemon

FOR THE FILLING
5 rounded tablespoonfuls golden syrup
4 oz fresh white breadcrumbs (110 g)
grated rind and juice of 1 lemon

Sift the flour and salt into a mixing bowl. Cut in the fat and crumble with your fingertips until the mixture looks like breadcrumbs. With a knife mix in the egg yolk and the grated rind and juice of 1 lemon. The mixture should just begin to stick together. If necessary add a very little cold water. Gather into a ball and if possible leave wrapped in the fridge for at least an hour. Heat the oven to Gas mark 6/400°F. Then knead the pastry a little on a floured board and roll out about $\frac{1}{8}$ in (3 mm) thick. Line a greased 8 in (20 cm) flan dish or pie plate with the pastry and prick the base lightly with a fork. Mix together the golden syrup, the breadcrumbs and the rind and juice of the second lemon. Pour over the pastry. Roll out the pastry trimmings and cut in strips to make a lattice pattern on top of the tart. Bake in the centre of the oven for 25–30 minutes. Serve hot or cold with cream.

Orange and Cream Cheese Tart (serves 8)

*This is similar to a cheese cake but more light and creamy
with a mild orange flavour, and is nice served warm.*

FOR THE PASTRY
6 oz strong flour (175 g)
1 heaped tablespoonful icing sugar
3 oz butter or margarine (75 g)
1 oz lard (25 g)

FOR THE FILLING
2 oz castor sugar (50 g)
8 oz cream cheese (225 g)
2 eggs – separated
3 tablespoonfuls single cream
finely grated rind of 1 orange
1 oz plain flour (25 g)
icing sugar

Make the pastry first. Sift the flour and icing sugar into a bowl. Cut in the fat, then
crumble in with your fingers until the mixture is like rough breadcrumbs. Add a
spot of very cold water and stir the mixture round with a knife until it just begins to
cling together. Then press into a ball with your hands, wrap in foil or plastic and
chill in the fridge for at least 30 minutes. Then roll out the pastry and line a greased
9–10 in. (23–25.5 cm) flan tin with a removable base. Cut the edges off neatly by
pressing the rolling pin over them. Prick the base lightly with a fork. Heat the oven
to Gas Mark 6/400°F.

To make the filling beat the sugar with the cream cheese until soft and smooth,
then beat in the egg yolks, one at a time, followed by the cream. Stir in the grated
orange peel and the flour. Whisk the egg whites until thick and fold them into the
cream cheese and yolk mixture. Pour into the pastry case. Cook in the centre of the
oven for 35–40 minutes until firm to a light touch in the centre. If the top seems to
be getting too brown lay a piece of foil gently over it. Leave the tart to cool a little in
the tin, then if necessary loosen the sides with a knife and turn out on to a serving
plate. I think it is nicest eaten lukewarm but you can serve it cold if you like, or if it
has become cold you can always heat it up gently in a low oven. Just before serving
dust the top with a little icing sugar through a fine sieve.

Lemon Tart with Chocolate Ginger Crust

When I first made this subtle tart with its sharp, mousse-like filling and crisp ginger chocolate crust I thought that it would be much preferred by the adults, but to my amazement both the children and adults had up to four helpings each!

FOR THE BISCUIT CRUST
7 oz ginger biscuits (200 g)
1½ oz butter (40 g)
1 dessertspoonful golden syrup
3 oz plain chocolate (75 g)

FOR THE FILLING
4 tablespoonfuls hot water
½ oz or 1 envelope of gelatine (10 g)
grated rind and juice of
2 large lemons
2 oz castor sugar (50 g)
½ pint double or whipping cream
(275 ml)
1 square plain chocolate

Lightly oil a 9–10 in (23–25.5 cm) shallow flan dish, preferably a metal one with a loose base. Grind the biscuits into crumbs either in a liquidiser or with a rolling pin. Melt the butter and golden syrup together in a pan, add the 3 oz (75 g) chocolate and stir until smooth. Add the biscuit crumbs and mix in thoroughly. Allow to cool slightly and then put the mixture into the flan dish and press very firmly down over the base and up the sides, smoothing with a metal spoon. Chill in the fridge for at least 2 hours until firm. If your flan dish has a loose base push the flan case out and put on to a serving plate before filling.

To make the lemon filling, put the hot water in a cup and sprinkle in the gelatine. Set the cup in a bowl of hot water and stir until dissolved. Leave the cup in the hot water. Grate the rinds of the lemons and put on one side. Squeeze the juice into a saucepan and stir in the castor sugar. Heat slightly and stir until the sugar has dissolved. Stir in the liquid gelatine. Then strain the juice out of the saucepan into a bowl and stir in the lemon rind. Leave until cool and beginning to set. Whisk the cream until thick but not stiff and stir thoroughly into the lemon mixture. Pour into the flan case and chill once more in the fridge until set. Grate the remaining square of chocolate on to the top.

Prune and Walnut Tart

This tart, which you serve cold, has a crisp biscuit pastry base, a tantalising filling and a creamy custard top.

FOR THE PASTRY
6 oz plain flour (175 g)
½ teaspoonful salt
3 oz icing sugar (75 g)
3 oz softened butter or margarine (75 g)
1 egg – whisked lightly

FOR THE FILLING
4 oz cream cheese (110 g)
1 rounded tablespoonful soft brown sugar
8 oz prunes (225 g)
2 oz walnuts – roughly chopped (50 g)

FOR THE CUSTARD TOP
2 eggs
1 oz castor sugar (25 g)
½ pint single cream (275 ml)

Several hours beforehand, or overnight, pour boiling water over the prunes and leave them to soak. To make the pastry, sift the flour, salt and icing sugar into a mixing bowl. Make a well in the centre and drop in the egg and the butter. Work together with your hands until blended; if the butter is really soft this will only take a minute. Then knead lightly with the palms of your hands until you have a smooth ball of dough. Leave in the fridge for at least 30 minutes.

To make the filling and top, remove the stones from the soaked prunes and roughly chop up the flesh. In a bowl mash the cream cheese with the brown sugar until soft. Thoroughly mix in the chopped prunes and nuts. Heat the oven to Gas Mark 5/375°F. Butter an 8½–9 in (21–23 cm) flan dish. Roll out the pastry and line the flan dish with it. Prick all over the bottom with a fork. Spread the prune mixture into the pastry case evenly. Whisk the eggs lightly with the sugar and then whisk in the cream. Pour this over the prune filling and put carefully into the centre of the oven. Bake for 35-40 minutes until the custard is set in the centre. A little sharp knife inserted should come out clean. Cool completely before serving.

Green Grape Tart

Towards the end of the summer, when the little seedless grapes are in season, I make this decorative and refreshing tart. The vanilla-flavoured French sweet pastry doesn't shrink or lose its shape during cooking and is like a crisp but melting biscuit in texture – but if you are in a hurry packet shortcrust pastry will do.

FOR THE PASTRY
4 oz plain flour (110 g)
2 oz soft margarine (50 g)
2 oz icing sugar (50 g)
1 large egg yolk
1 teaspoonful vanilla essence

FOR THE FILLING
4 oz full cream cheese (110 g)
2 oz castor sugar (50 g)
juice of ½ lemon
¾ lb seedless green grapes (350 g)
3—4 rounded tablespoonfuls lemon
jelly or lime marmalade

To make the pastry, sift the flour on to a cool surface and make a well in the centre. Put the other ingredients in the centre and work them together with the fingertips of one hand. Then draw the flour into the mixture and when it is all worked in, knead lightly until smooth with the palm of your hand. Form into a ball, wrap in plastic or foil and chill in the fridge for at least 30 minutes. Heat the oven to Gas Mark 6/400°F. Roll out the pastry and line a greased 9–10 in (23–25.5 cm) loose-bottomed flan dish with it. Prick the bottom with a fork and then lay on a piece of greaseproof paper or foil filled with dry beans or rice. Bake in the centre of the oven for 15–20 minutes. Cool and then carefully turn the pastry case out of the flan dish on to a serving plate. Beat the cream cheese with the castor sugar until smooth and then beat in the lemon juice. Spread the mixture over the bottom of the pastry case. Arrange the grapes on the top. Then gently melt the lemon jelly marmalade in a pan and spoon it over the grapes. Chill before serving.

Quince Lattice Tart (serves 8)

If you are lucky enough to have a quince tree in your garden or if you know of anyone who does, you may already have made good use of this fruit's exquisite scent and flavour. But jelly and jam is by no means all you can do with them. Did you know that they are delicious stewed with spiced lamb or pork?

This pretty tart with its rich sweet pastry and crispy glazed top is to me made perfect by the pinky orange filling of puréed quinces. However, you can of course use cooking apples instead if you have to, but in that case stew them with less sugar as they will be far less sour than the quinces.

FOR THE PASTRY
8 oz strong plain flour (225 g)
2 rounded tablespoonfuls icing sugar
4 oz butter or margarine (110 g)
3 oz lard (75 g)

FOR THE FILLING
1¼–1½ lb quinces (560–700 g)
4 oz demerara sugar (110 g)
juice of 1 large orange
1–2 oz butter (25–50 g)
2 eggs
2 oz ground almonds (50 g)
1 level tablespoonful castor sugar
1 teaspoonful ground mace or cinnamon

First make the pastry. Sift the flour and icing sugar into a bowl. Cut in the fat and crumble with your fingers until the mixture resembles rough breadcrumbs. Now add literally only a spot, about 2 teaspoonfuls, of very cold water and stir into the mixture with a knife until it starts to stick together. Press the mixture into a ball, wrap in plastic or foil and chill in the fridge for at least an hour.

Meanwhile, peel, core and cut the quinces into chunks. Put them into a saucepan with the demerara sugar and the orange juice. Cover and simmer gently for 20–30 minutes until soft and mushy. Stir in the butter until melted. Cool the mixture slightly and then whizz in a liquidiser until smooth. Allow to cool completely.

Heat the oven to Gas Mark 5/357°F. Butter a 9½–10 in (24–25.5 cm) shallow flan dish, preferably the metal kind with a loose base. Cut off a little over half the pastry, knead slightly, shape into a ball and roll out on a floured board into a circle big enough to line the flan dish. Press the rolling pin over the edges to cut off the excess pastry neatly. Prick lightly with a fork. Whisk one whole egg and one egg yolk (reserving the white) into the quince purée. Then stir in the ground almonds. Spoon the mixture into the flan case. Roll out the remaining pastry and cut into thin strips. Arrange the strips closely together in a lattice pattern, re-rolling the pastry if necessary and leaving the edges hanging over. When finished, press the rolling pin round the edges to cut off the overlapping pieces. Add the castor sugar and the mace to the reserved egg white and whisk together lightly with a fork. Brush thickly all over the lattice top and bake in the centre of the oven for 40–45 minutes until rich golden brown. Serve warm or cold with cream.

Cider Apple Tart

On holiday in Devon during the autumn we always have a profusion of apples and lots of very good cider so that I have to think up all sorts of ways to use both. This tangy tart is popular.

FOR THE BISCUIT CRUST
5–6 oz ginger or other sweet
crunchy biscuits (150–175 g)
1½ oz butter or margarine (40 g)

FOR THE FILLING
grated rind and juice of 2 large lemons
about ½ pint medium cider (275 ml)
1 oz cornflour (25 g)
3 oz castor sugar plus a little more (75 g)
2–3 cooking apples
6 fl oz whipping cream (150–
175 ml)

Grease a 7½–8 in (19–20 cm) flan dish, preferably with a push-up base so that you can turn the tart out. Crush the biscuits in a plastic bag with a rolling pin or in a liquidiser. Melt the butter and stir the crushed biscuits into it. Using a metal spoon, press this mixture firmly over the base and sides of the flan dish.

Put the grated lemon rind on one side and squeeze out the juice into a measuring jug making it up to ¾ pint (425 ml) by adding cider. Blend the cornflour with a little of the juices until smooth and then add to the rest of the juice. Pour into a saucepan, add 3 oz (75 g) of castor sugar and bring to the boil, stirring all the time. Bubble for 2–3 minutes until you have a thick paste. Add the grated lemon rind and pour the mixture into the biscuit flan crust. Heat the oven to Gas Mark 5/375°F. Peel the apples and slice thinly. Arrange the slices neatly on top of the lemon cider mixture. Sprinkle all over with castor sugar and bake in the centre of the oven for about 30 minutes or until the apples are soft. Cool. When cold whip the cream until thick and spoon on top of the apples. Chill until ready to serve.

Tarte Tatin

In France this upside down apple pie is eaten specially at Christmas time. The buttery caramelised taste of the apples and the rich sweet pastry are delectable.

FOR THE PASTRY
6 oz strong plain flour (175 g)
½ teaspoonful salt
3 oz castor sugar (75 g)
3 oz softened butter or margarine (75 g)
1 egg – lightly whisked

FOR THE FILLING
2 oz butter (50 g)
6 oz castor sugar (175 g)
1½ lb cooking apples (700 g) – 2 lb
(900 g) if your flan dish is more than
1 in (2.5 cm) deep

Make the pastry beforehand. Sift the flour, sugar and salt into a bowl. Make a well in the centre and put in the butter and the whisked egg. Work into the flour with your fingertips until the mixture is well blended. Then knead lightly until smooth. Gather into a ball and leave to rest in the fridge for at least an hour.

Then heat the oven to Gas Mark 6/400°F. Smear the butter over the bottom and sides of an 8–9 in (20–23 cm) flan dish (not one with a loose base). Then speckle the sugar over the butter on the bottom. Peel and core the apples, slice thinly and arrange neatly all over the sugar. Roll the pastry into a circle very slightly larger than the flan dish. Moisten the edge of the dish and lay the pastry on top. Cut the excess pastry off neatly by pressing the rolling pin round the edges. Prick all over with a fork. Bake just above the centre of the oven until golden brown – about 25 minutes. Then lay a piece of foil on top and continue cooking for another 10 minutes. Turn out of the flan dish on to a large round plate. Sprinkle another heaped tablespoonful of sugar over the apples and bubble under a hot grill for 3–5 minutes until browned. Serve hot. The French serve their slightly sharp "crème fraîche" with this (see page 155).

Cranberry Tart

The brilliant red fresh cranberries which fill the shops towards Christmas are often only used for cranberry sauce. This tart is much enhanced by their sharp, distinctive flavour.

FOR THE CRUST
6 oz ginger biscuits – crumbled (175 g)
2 oz butter – melted (50 g)
1 heaped tablespoonful soft brown sugar or demerara sugar

FOR THE FILLING
½ oz cornflour (10 g)
1 pint milk (570 ml)
4–5 strips lemon rind
1–2 oz castor sugar (25–50 g)
2 tablespoonfuls double cream

FOR THE CRANBERRY TOP
5 oz granulated sugar (150 g)
6 fl oz water (175 ml)
½ teaspoonful ground ginger
½ lb cranberries (225 g)
1 oz blanched split almonds (25 g)

First cook the cranberries. Dissolve the sugar in the water over a low heat, bring to the boil, add the cranberries and simmer fairly rapidly for 8 minutes. Stir in the ground ginger. Leave to get completely cold.

To make the flan crust crumble the ginger biscuits either in a liquidiser or by crushing them with a rolling pin. Mix into them the brown sugar and the melted butter. Line an 8–9 in (20–23 cm) shallow flan dish with the mixture, patting it firmly and smoothly with a metal spoon. Put it in a pre-heated oven at Gas Mark 5/375°F for 5 minutes.

To make the filling blend the cornflour to a smooth cream in a bowl with 1–2 tablespoonfuls of the milk. Bring the remaining milk to the boil with the lemon rind. Strain it on to the blended mixture, stirring well. Return to the saucepan and bring to the boil, stirring all the time until the mixture thickens. Cook for a further 2–3 minutes and add castor sugar to taste. Stir in the cream. Pour the mixture into the crumbled biscuit flan case. Allow to cool. Keep it cold in the fridge and not more than an hour before you want to eat it, spoon the cranberry mixture all over the top and decorate with a pattern of split almonds.

Jellied Gooseberry Flan

Jellies made with fresh fruit are wonderfully refreshing. This is a tangy mixture of whole gooseberries and apricots on a spongy base, and it's very easy to make!

FOR THE JELLY
1 lb fresh gooseberries – topped
and tailed (450 g)
¾ lb fresh apricots – halved and
stoned (350 g)
4–5 oz granulated sugar (110–150 g)
juice of 2 oranges
2 packets or 1 oz gelatine (25 g)

FOR THE BASE
3 oz butter or margarine (75 g)
1 rounded tablespoonful of apricot
or gooseberry jam
8 trifle sponges

TO DECORATE
chopped crystallised ginger or nuts

Put the fruit, the sugar and the orange juice into a pan. Add enough water to almost cover the fruit. Bring to the boil and simmer for about 10 minutes until soft. Dissolve the gelatine in 3 tablespoonfuls of hot water and stir into the fruit mixture. Pour into a round 2-pint (1-litre) dish, cool and then allow to set in the fridge.

Melt the butter with the jam. Crumble the trifle sponges roughly in a bowl and stir in the melted butter and jam to bind the crumble together. Pile the mixture all over the top of the set jelly, smooth and put back in the fridge for at least 30 minutes.

To turn out dip the dish in hot water for a moment or two, then loosen the sides with a knife and, giving it a good shake, turn out on to a serving plate. Sometimes the sponge base may come out first. Don't worry, just turn the jelly out on top of it. Decorate the jelly top with chopped ginger. Serve with cream.

Glazed Strawberry Flan

This beautiful glossy flan with a light sponge base will enhance any summer meal or party.

FOR THE BASE
3 oz plain flour (75 g)
1½ level teaspoonfuls baking powder
3 large eggs
3 oz castor sugar (75 g)
½ teaspoonful almond essence
pinch of salt

FOR THE TOPPING
1–1¼ lb fresh strawberries (450–560 g)
about ¾ jar redcurrant jelly
juice of ½ lemon

Grease a 10 in (25.5 cm) flan dish and line the bottom with a disc of greased greaseproof paper. Heat the oven to Gas Mark 5/375°F. Sift the flour, baking powder and salt together two or three times and put on one side. Put the eggs and sugar into a deep bowl over a pan of hot water and whisk with an electric or hand whisk until the mixture becomes thick and retains the impression of the whisk when you pull it out. Add the essence and whisk in. Take the bowl off the pan of water. Gently fold in the sifted flour with a metal spoon. Spoon the mixture into the flan dish and cook in the centre of the oven for about 15 minutes until the mixture has turned a light brown and is springy to touch in the centre. Lay a folded teacloth on a cooling rack. Carefully loosen the sides with a knife and turn out on to the cloth. Peel off the greaseproof paper. When cool, put a serving plate or cakeboard on the flan base and turn upside down with the help of the cooling rack. Now halve the strawberries and arrange neatly all over the flan. Melt the redcurrant jelly with the lemon juice in a pan and spoon it over the strawberries, spreading some on the sides of the flan too.

Green Grape Flan

When the strawberry season is over this flan can be made with little seedless grapes which come into the shops during the late summer. If they are out of season you can cut large ones in half and flick out the pips.

FOR THE BASE
3 large eggs
3 oz castor sugar (75 g)
½ teaspoon lemon or almond essence
3 oz plain flour (75 g)
1½ level teaspoonfuls baking powder
pinch of salt

FOR THE TOPPING
about 1½ lb green grapes (700 g)
about ¾ jar of lime marmalade
juice of ½ lemon

Grease a 10 in (25.5 cm) flan dish. Line the bottom with a disc of greased greaseproof paper. Heat the oven to Gas Mark 5/375°F. Sift the flour, baking powder and salt together two or three times and put on one side. Put the eggs and sugar into a deep bowl over a pan of hot water and whisk with an electric or hand whisk until the mixture stands in soft peaks. Add the essence and remove the bowl from the hot water. Gently fold in the sifted flour with a metal spoon. Spoon the mixture into the flan dish and cook in the centre of the oven for about 15 minutes until light golden brown and springy to touch in the centre. Lay a folded teacloth on a cooling rack. Carefully loosen the sides of the flan with a knife and turn out on to the cloth. Peel off the paper. When cool, put a large round plate or cake board on top of the flan and turn upside down with the help of the cooling rack. Now arrange the grapes in neat circles all over the sponge. Melt the lime marmalade with the lemon juice and spoon it over the grapes, spreading it over the sides of the sponge too. Cool and serve with cream.

GÂTEAUX AND PUDDING CAKES

Putney Peaches and Cream

Simply fresh peaches and cream on a smooth spongy cinnamon base, topped with crunchy nuts. Very easily made and a good way to make a few peaches feed many mouths.

FOR THE BASE
2 oz plain flour (50 g)
½ oz cornflour (10 g)
1 teaspoonful ground cinnamon
1 level teaspoonful baking powder
pinch of salt
2 oz icing sugar (50 g)
1 large egg – separated
3 tablespoonfuls water
3 tablespoonfuls sunflower oil

FOR THE TOPPING
3 peaches
5–6 fl oz double or whipping cream (150–175 ml)
1 tablespoonful castor sugar
1–2 oz chopped hazelnuts (25–50 g)

Heat the oven to Gas Mark 5/375°F and lightly oil a 2–2½-pint (1–1½-litre) ovenproof dish. Sift the flours, cinnamon, baking powder, salt and icing sugar into a bowl. In a cup, mix together the egg yolk, water and oil with a fork and stir into the sifted ingredients. Whisk or beat to a smooth batter. Whisk the egg white until stiff and fold into the batter. Transfer to the buttered dish and bake in the centre of the oven for 20–25 minutes until risen and golden brown. Cool. When cold, whisk the cream until thick and whisk in the castor sugar. Slice the peaches thinly and mix into the cream. Spoon the mixture on to the cake base and sprinkle chopped nuts on top. Chill until ready to eat.

Upside Down Apple and Caramel Cake

Another good way to use cooking apples. This is a tender white cake, gooey with apples on top and covered with dark caramel custard.

FOR THE TOPPING
butter or margarine
2 plus 1 rounded tablespoonfuls
castor sugar
1 lb cooking apples (450 g)

FOR THE CAKE
6 oz plain flour (175 g)
2 level teaspoonfuls baking powder
½ teaspoonful salt
3 fl oz sunflower, groundnut or
corn oil (75 ml)
3 fl oz water (75 ml)
2 fl oz milk (55 ml)

1 teaspoonful vanilla essence
2 egg whites
pinch of cream of tartar
6 oz castor sugar (175 g)

FOR THE CUSTARD
2 oz castor sugar (50 g)
2 egg yolks
4 tablespoonfuls single cream
2 tablespoonfuls lemon juice
a few chopped nuts

Generously butter an 8–9 in (20-23 cm) cake tin spreading it especially thickly over the base. Evenly sprinkle the base with 2 rounded tablespoonfuls of the sugar. Peel, core and slice the apples thinly and arrange them in an overlapping pattern on top of the sugar in the cake tin. Sprinkle over the third tablespoonful of sugar. Heat the oven to Gas Mark 4/350°F. Sift the flour, baking powder and salt into a bowl. Add the oil, water, milk and vanilla essence and beat to a rather thick, smooth batter. Whisk the egg whites until foamy, add the cream of tartar and whisk until stiff but not breaking up. Whisk in 6 oz (175 g) castor sugar a bit at a time. Fold this meringue-like mixture into the batter with a metal spoon and pour on top of the apples. Cook in the centre of the oven for 45–50 minutes. Leave to cool a little in the tin, then turn out upside down on to a serving plate.

Dissolve another 2 oz (50 g) sugar in 2 tablespoonfuls of water in a pan over a low heat. Then bring to the boil and bubble fiercely, without stirring, until pale golden brown. Remove from the heat and stir in the single cream and then the reserved egg yolks. Return to a low heat (don't boil) for a moment or two to thicken the custard a little more and stir in the lemon juice. Cool slightly and spread over the apples, letting it dribble over the edges. Sprinkle over a few chopped nuts. Eat lukewarm or cold with cream.

Apricot Tease

The odd name for this recipe was thought up by my husband. I made the pudding, a sort of inverted cheesecake, for a family lunch one weekend and as I didn't know what to call it he made the suggestion because he claimed the pudding was so good that even after a filling Sunday lunch it teased the appetite once more!

8 oz dried apricots – soaked in
water for several hours (225 g)
2 oz soft brown sugar (50 g)
1 pint water (570 ml)
juice of 1 lemon
1 packet or ½ oz gelatine (10 g)
1 packet trifle sponges or some old
sponge cake
8 oz curd or cream cheese (225 g)
1–2 oz castor sugar (25-50 g)
¼ pint double or whipping cream (150 ml)
½–1 oz almond flakes (10–25 g)

Simmer the soaked apricots with the brown sugar and lemon juice in the water in a covered pan for 30–45 minutes until very soft. Then sprinkle in the gelatine and stir round until dissolved. Pour into a 2–2½-pint (1–1½-litre) capacity round dish or cake tin. Cover the top with the sponges, cutting them to fit the dish and pressing them only very slightly down to touch the hot apricot mixture. Cool and then chill well in the fridge. To turn out, dip the dish briefly in hot water until, when giving a good shake, the contents will drop out on to a serving plate.

Put the curd cheese into a bowl with the castor sugar to taste and beat together until soft. In another bowl whisk the cream until thick and then fold it into the softened curd cheese. Ice the apricot cake thickly all over with this mixture, smoothing it with a wide knife in rough flicks. Chill again in the fridge before serving. Meanwhile, spread the flaked almonds on a plate and put them in a medium to hot oven for a few minutes until golden brown. Cool and sprinkle these crisply roasted almonds over the cake just before serving.

BOP—4 **

Almond Cheese Cake

This is more like a European cheese cake than an American one which means that
it is more like a cake, but it isn't at all heavy and is most suitable as a pudding.

1 oz fresh white breadcrumbs (25 g)
a little butter
3 eggs
3 oz castor sugar (75 g)
8 oz curd cheese (225 g)
½ teaspoonful almond essence
(optional)
2 oz ground almonds (50 g)
1 oz candied peel (25 g)
2 oz sultanas (50 g)
grated rind of 1 lemon
1 oz self-raising flour (25 g)
1 carton soured cream
a few roasted almonds (optional)

Heat the oven to Gas Mark 4/350°F. Spread the breadcrumbs on a plate in the
oven for 10–15 minutes until crisp. Then leave the oven on and butter a loose-
bottomed 6–7 in (15–18 cm) cake tin, spreading the butter more thickly on the
bottom. Sprinkle the breadcrumbs evenly over the bottom. Whisk the eggs and
sugar together until pale and frothy. Beat in the cheese and essence until smooth
and then beat in the ground almonds. Stir in the peel, sultanas, the lemon rind and
lastly the flour. Pour the mixture into the cake tin and cook in the centre of the oven
for about 45 minutes until firm. Allow to cool and turn out of the tin on to a serving
plate. Spread the soured cream all over the cake and chill in the fridge. If liked,
sprinkle the top with roasted flaked almonds before serving.

Walnut Spice Gâteau

A great favourite! It is a deliciously nutty cake but at the same time very light and both quick and easy to make. Sandwiched together with cream and shiny with a sharp jellied glaze it is a perfect finale to any meal.

3 oz plain flour (75 g)
1½ teaspoonfuls baking powder
1 level teaspoonful mixed spice
¼ teaspoonful salt
3 large eggs
3 oz soft brown sugar (75 g)
2 oz chopped walnuts (50 g)
¼ pint double or whipping
cream – whipped until thick (150 ml)
1 tablespoonful orange or
redcurrant jelly
2 teaspoonfuls lemon juice or water
a few halved walnuts to decorate the top

Lightly oil two 7–8 in (18–20 cm) sandwich tins and line each with a disc of oiled greaseproof paper. Heat the oven to Gas Mark 4/350°F. Sift the flour with the baking powder, spice and salt two or three times and put on one side. Put the eggs into a deep bowl standing over a large pan of hot water. Whisk until thickish and pale lemon-coloured. Then whisk in the brown sugar and continue whisking until the mixture is greatly increased in volume and thick enough to stand in peaks. (Of course this is all much quicker if you use an electric whisk.) Then, using a metal spoon, very lightly fold in the chopped walnuts. Sprinkle the sifted flour on top and gently cut and fold into the mixture. Pour into the prepared tins and bake in the centre of the oven for 15–20 minutes until risen and well browned.

Allow to cool in the tins, then loosen the sides with a knife and turn out. Put on to a serving plate and sandwich together with the whipped cream. Gently melt the jelly (I once used home-made quince jelly which was delicious) with the lemon juice until smooth. Brush over the top of the cake and decorate with a pattern of walnut halves. Keep in a cool place, preferably not the fridge unless you are saving it until next day, in which case take it out for at least 30 minutes before serving.

Orange Blossom Cake

This cake has a particularly smooth, light texture which goes well with the delicate flavour of the orange flower water. As it is made with oil instead of butter there is no creaming to do and it's very quick to make. In the summer it looks lovely decorated with little white or yellow flowers from the garden.

5 oz plain flour (150 g)
1 oz cornflour (25 g)
2 level teaspoonfuls baking powder
½ teaspoonful salt
5 oz icing sugar (150 g)
3 fl oz sunflower or ground nut oil (75 ml)
3 fl oz water (75 ml)
2 large eggs – separated
1 tablespoon plus 2 teaspoonfuls
concentrated orange flower water
(available at chemists and delicatessens)
finely grated peel of 1 orange
½ pint double or whipping cream (275 ml)
chopped nuts or grated orange peel to decorate

Heat oven to Gas Mark 5/375°F. Oil two 7–8 in (18–20 cm) sandwich tins and line with discs of oiled greaseproof paper. Sift the dry ingredients together into a bowl. Mix the oil and water and the egg yolks together with a fork, add to the dry mixture and beat to a smooth batter. Stir in 1 tablespoonful of the flower water and the grated orange rind. Whisk the egg whites until they stand in peaks and fold gently into the batter with a metal spoon. Pour into the cake tins and bake in the centre of the oven for 25–30 minutes until well risen and golden. Leave in the tins for about 10 minutes, then loosen the sides with a knife and turn out on to a cooling rack.

When cool, whisk the cream until thick and then whisk in 2 teaspoonfuls of the flower water. Sandwich the cake together with half the cream and put the rest on top of the cake. Decorate with a little grated orange rind, chopped nuts or fresh flowers.

Chocolate Peach Crumb Cake (serves 8–10)

Using breadcrumbs instead of flour and adding marmalade to the mixture gives this pudding cake a lovely gooey consistency and a good strong flavour. This recipe uses fresh peaches as the fruit but of course you can use any soft fruit you like: raspberries are specially delicious. In winter use dessert pears. The cake part of the pudding actually improves if made one or two days beforehand.

FOR THE CAKE
4 oz plain chocolate (110 g)
2 rounded tablespoonfuls marmalade
2 tablespoonfuls water
4 oz butter or margarine (110 g)
3 oz castor or soft brown sugar (75 g)

3 eggs – separated
4 oz fresh white breadcrumbs (110 g)
pinch of salt
¼ pint double or whipping cream (150 ml)

FOR THE TOPPING
3–4 peaches – stoned and sliced finely
3 oz plain chocolate (75 g)
2 tablespoonfuls water
1 oz butter or margarine (25 g)

Grease and line the base of two 7–8 in (18–20 cm) sandwich tins with discs of greased greaseproof paper. Heat oven to Gas Mark 4/350°F. Gently melt the chocolate with the water and marmalade. Put on one side. Cream the butter and sugar until light and fluffy. Beat in the egg yolks and then stir in the melted chocolate mixture and the breadcrumbs. Whisk the egg whites with a pinch of salt until thick and fold into the chocolate mixture. Pour into the prepared tins and bake in the centre of the oven for 25–30 minutes or until springy to a light touch in the centre of each cake.

Leave the cakes in the tins for about 10 minutes, then loosen the sides carefully with a knife and turn out on to a rack to cool. When cool, whip the cream until thick. Spread half of it on each cake, put one cake on a serving dish and sprinkle half the sliced peaces on top of the cream. Put the other cake on top with its cream side down. Arrange the rest of the peaches neatly on top of the cake. Melt the remaining 3 oz (75 g) chocolate with 2 tablespoonfuls of water, then add the butter and stir until smooth. Cool slightly and spoon roughly over the peaches. Chill in the fridge before serving.

Hazel Fruit Sandwich

A light but gooey half cake, half meringue made with crunchy hazelnuts and whites of egg, filled with a sharp orange custard, fresh strawberries and whipped cream. It's a mouthwatering summer pudding, but can also be a lovely treat in winter using sliced bananas instead of the strawberries.

FOR THE CAKE
4 egg whites
½ teaspoonful cream of tartar
pinch of salt
1 tablespoonful cold water
5 oz castor sugar (150 g)
1 teaspoonful vanilla essence
1 oz cornflour (25 g)
1 oz ground hazelnuts or
almonds (25 g)
1 oz chopped hazelnuts (25 g)

FOR THE FILLING AND TOP
4 egg yolks
grated rind and juice of 1 orange
juice of 1 lemon
1 oz sugar (25 g)
6–8 oz fresh strawberries,
raspberries or bananas (175–225 g)
6 fl oz double or whipping
cream – whisked until stiff (175 ml)
1 oz chopped hazelnuts (25 g)

Heat oven to Gas Mark 1/275°F. Put a disc of greaseproof paper on the bottom of an ungreased 7–8 in (18–20 cm) cake tin. Put the egg whites, cream of tartar, salt and cold water in a bowl and whisk until stiff. Using a metal spoon fold in the sugar a tablespoonful at a time and add the essence. Add the cornflour through a fine sieve and fold in. Then lightly fold in the ground hazelnuts and lastly 1 oz (25 g) chopped hazelnuts. Pour into the prepared tin and bake towards the bottom of the oven for 1¼–1½ hours until springy to touch in the centre.

While the cake is cooking make the orange custard. Put the egg yolks, orange rind and juice, lemon juice and sugar into the top of a double saucepan or into a bowl set over a pan of water. Cook over gently simmering water, stirring with a wooden spoon until the custard thickens. This won't take long. Leave to get cold.

When the cake is cooked leave in the tin until cold, then loosen the sides with a knife and turn out. Using a sharp knife cut the cake carefully in half. Put the bottom half on a plate and spread with the custard. Put the strawberries on top of the custard and then half of the whipped cream. Then put on the other half of the cake and spread the remaining cream on top, smoothing with a knife. Sprinkle all over with chopped hazelnuts and chill in the fridge before serving.

St. Clement's Cake

This very light "oranges and lemons" cake, made with semolina and ground almonds instead of flour, has a slightly crunchy texture.

3 large eggs – separated
grated rind and juice of 1 lemon
4 oz castor sugar (110 g)
2 oz fine semolina (50 g)
1 oz ground almonds (25 g)
½ teaspoonful cream of tartar
¼ pint double or whipping cream (150 ml)
2 tablespoonfuls plain yoghurt
3—4 tablespoonfuls chunky marmalade

Heat the oven to Gas Mark 4/350°F. Lightly oil a 7–8 in (18–20 cm) cake tin and line with a disc of oiled greaseproof paper. Grate the lemon rind and put on one side. Put the egg yolks, castor sugar and lemon juice into a bowl and beat until pale. Now add the semolina, ground almonds and the lemon rind and stir all together thoroughly. Whisk the egg whites with the cream of tartar until they stand in soft peaks. Then pour the yolk mixture on to the whites and lightly fold in with a metal spoon. Pour the mixture into the prepared cake tin and bake in the centre of the oven for 40–50 minutes or until springy to a light touch in the centre. Leave in the tin for 10 minutes, then loosen the edges with a knife and turn out. When cool, cut in half. Whip the cream until stiff, stir in the yoghurt and sandwich the cake together with this mixture. Then slightly melt the marmalade and spread on top of the cake.

Hazelnut Shortcake Sandwich

A rich and tender shortcake gâteau which is incredibly quick and easy to make. During the summer it can be a thrilling treat, filled with fresh soft fruit instead of jam.

2 oz roasted hazelnuts (50 g)
8 oz butter (225 g)
scant 3 oz soft brown sugar (75 g)
8 oz plain flour (225 g)
good apricot jam
¼ pint double or whipping cream (150 ml)
a little icing sugar

If not using ready-chopped roasted hazelnuts, chop up whole hazelnuts and roast on a baking sheet in a medium to high oven for a few minutes until brown. Grease two 7–8 in (18–20 cm) sandwich tins. Heat the oven to Gas Mark 6/400°F. Beat the butter until soft, then stir in the sugar and flour with a wooden spoon until thoroughly mixed. Stir in the roasted hazelnuts. Spoon the dough (it will be rather too sticky to handle successfully) equally between the two tins and then, using floured hands, press lightly and evenly over the bottom of the tins. Bake in the centre of the oven for about 20 minutes, until golden brown. Leave to cool a little in the tins, then loosen the edges if necessary and turn out gently on to a cooling rack. When cool put one circle on a serving plate and spread generously with the apricot jam. Then whip the cream until thick and spread over the jam. Top with the second circle and sprinkle the top all over with icing sugar through a sieve. Keep in a cool place but not the fridge until ready to serve.

Liza's Lemon Pudding

So called because it's my older daughter's favourite, this is an extra light pudding cake, filled with a refreshing mixture of whipped cream and yoghurt and covered with a sharp lemon syrup.

FOR THE CAKE
4 oz self-raising flour (110 g)
5 oz castor sugar (150 g)
½ teaspoonful salt
4 tablespoonfuls sunflower, ground nut or corn oil
3 eggs – separated
5 tablespoonfuls water
½ teaspoonful vanilla essence
grated rind of 1 lemon
½ teaspoonful cream of tartar

FOR THE SYRUP
Juice of 1 lemon
2 tablespoonfuls water
4 oz sugar (110 g)

FOR THE FILLING
1 small carton double cream
1½ tablespoonfuls plain yoghurt

Pre-heat the oven to Gas Mark 3/325°F. Have ready an ungreased deep ring tin or charlotte mould. (If you don't have a ring tin you can do this pudding in two sandwich tins and then sandwich the cakes together with the filling.) Sift together the flour, sugar and salt. Make a well in the centre and add the oil, egg yolks, water, vanilla essence and lemon peel. Beat or whisk until the batter is smooth. Add the cream of tartar to the egg whites and beat until they stand in peaks. Pour the batter on to the egg whites and fold in gently with a metal spoon, taking care not to stir the mixture. Pour into the tin and bake in the centre of the oven for 1¼ hours. Leave in the tin until cold. To remove the pudding loosen the edges all round with a knife and tap the base of the tin sharply. Put on to a serving dish. Put the lemon juice, water and sugar into a saucepan and dissolve over a low heat. Bring to the boil and bubble fiercely for 2–4 minutes until slightly thicker. Pour the syrup all over the pudding. Whip up the cream until thick. Then stir in the yoghurt and fill the middle of the ring with the mixture. Keep in a cool place, but not in the fridge, until ready to serve.

Primrose Cake

This is a very soft and light half-cake, half-mousse which I call "Primrose" because the crumb is such a pretty pale primrose yellow. In fact the flavour is lemony, like a deliciously mild lemon curd, and the cake is iced all over with whipped cream. In the spring you can make it a genuine primrose cake and also extremely decorative by arranging fresh primroses all over the cake on top of the whipped cream. Primroses are, incidentally, perfectly edible.

3 eggs – separated
5 oz castor sugar (150 g)
grated rind and juice of 1 lemon
1 oz cornflour (25 g)
1 oz self-raising flour (25 g)
¼ teaspoonful cream of tartar
good pinch of salt
¼ pint double or whipping cream (150 ml)
fresh primroses (optional)

Heat the oven to Gas Mark 4/350°F. Lightly grease a 7–8 in (18–20 cm) cake tin and line with a disc of greased greaseproof paper. Whisk the egg yolks with the castor sugar until very pale. Whisk in the rind and juice of the lemon. Sift the flour and cornflour on to the mixture and stir in. Whisk the egg whites with the cream of tartar and salt until stiff and then, using a metal spoon, fold gently but thoroughly into the yolk mixture. Pour into the prepared tin and bake in the centre of the oven for 35–40 minutes until well risen and firm to a light touch in the centre. Then cool in the tin and don't worry if the cake sinks a bit, that's normal. Loosen the sides of the cake with a knife and turn out on to a serving plate. Whisk the cream until thick and ice the cake all over in rough flicks. Chill in the fridge until ready to serve. During the spring the cake can then be decorated with fresh primroses and even a few violets and will look wonderful.

Nina's Drenched Lemon Cake

A friend of mine looks dreamy as she remembers her mother making this moist tangy cake during her childhood. It is certainly a perfect family pudding, being simple to make and extremely popular with everyone.

6 oz butter or margarine (175 g)
6 oz soft brown sugar (175 g)
3 eggs
grated rind and juice of 2 lemons
6 oz self-raising wholemeal or
farmhouse flour (175 g)
1 rounded teaspoonful baking powder
pinch of salt
3–4 tablespoonfuls milk
2 oz granulated sugar (50 g)

Heat the oven to Gas Mark 4/350°F. Butter a 6–7 in (15–18 cm), deep cake tin and line with a disc of buttered greaseproof paper. Cream the butter and sugar until fluffy. Beat in the eggs thoroughly, one at a time. Grate the lemon rind on to the mixture. Mix the salt and baking powder with the flour and fold it into the mixture together with the grated rind. Stir in enough milk to give a soft dropping consistency. Put into the cake tin and smooth the top. Bake in the centre of the oven for 40–50 minutes until springy to touch in the centre. Loosen the sides with a knife and turn the cake out on to a serving plate right side up. Skewer holes in the top of the cake, piercing right through to the bottom. Put the granulated sugar and the lemon juice into a pan and bring to the boil, stirring to dissolve the sugar, and then bubble fiercely for 30 seconds. Pour the syrup slowly over the top of the cake, letting it seep into the holes. Serve warm or cold with cream.

Feather Pudding

Few people will guess that this very light and moist pudding cake is made with carrots. Carrots, being sweet, are an old-established ingredient in puddings. They are rarely used nowadays, in spite of their beautiful colour, their good flavour and texture and of course their low cost. This pudding has a lemon-sharp topping of bright orange candied carrots which makes it look very pretty.

FOR THE CAKE
4 oz self-raising flour (110 g)
½ teaspoonful salt
6 oz castor sugar (175 g)
4 tablespoonfuls sunflower, ground nut or corn oil
5 tablespoonfuls water
1 teaspoonful vanilla essence
3 large eggs – separated
8 oz carrots – finely grated (225 g)
1 level teaspoonful cream of tartar

FOR THE CANDIED CARROT TOPPING
8 oz carrots (225 g)
1 lemon
8 oz sugar (225 g)
4 tablespoonfuls water

Heat the oven to Gas Mark 3/325°F. Line an oiled 7–8 in (18–20 cm) cake tin with oiled greaseproof paper. Sieve together into a mixing bowl the flour, salt and castor sugar. Add the oil, water, vanilla essence and the egg yolks. Beat or whisk thoroughly until you have a smooth batter. Stir in the grated carrot. In a large bowl whisk the egg whites with the cream of tartar until they stand in soft peaks. Pour the batter gradually on to the egg whites and fold in gently with a metal spoon. Transfer to the prepared cake tin and bake in the centre of the oven for about 1½ hours or until a sharp knife inserted in the cake comes out clean.

Meanwhile make the topping. Peel and slice the carrots and chop into very small cubes. Coarsely grate the lemon peel and squeeze out the juice. Put the carrots, lemon peel and juice, the sugar and water into a saucepan and boil fiercely for 5–10 minutes until setting point is reached – when a blob of the syrup on a cold plate sets or 220°F is reached on a sugar thermometer. Leave on one side in the saucepan. When the cake is cooked leave to cool in the tin for about 10 minutes, then loosen the edges with a knife and turn out on to a wire rack to cool. When cool put on to a serving plate and spread the candied carrots over the top. If the syrup has become too stiff, reheat a little just to make it spreadable and let it cool again before serving with cream.

Hazelnut and Walnut Gâteau

This glossy pudding cake has a crunchy but light texture. It is most delicious served with some sharp-tasting stewed dried apricots. If you have a ring-mould tin you can bake the mixture in that and stuff the middle with fresh fruit and whipped cream.

4 oz butter (110 g)
5 oz castor sugar (150 g)
1 teaspoonful vanilla essence
3 large eggs – lightly beaten
3 oz ground hazelnuts (75 g) – you can
grind whole hazelnuts up in a
second in a liquidiser or coffee grinder
3 oz candied peel (75 g)
3 oz shelled walnuts (75 g)
1½ oz plain flour (40 g)
1 teaspoonful baking powder
pinch of salt
2–3 tablespoonfuls redcurrant jelly
or jelly marmalade
a few whole hazelnuts and walnuts
and some demerara sugar to decorate

Grease and flour a fairly deep 7 in (18 cm) cake tin. Pre-heat the oven to Gas Mark 4/350°F. Put a disc of greaseproof paper on the bottom. Cream the butter and sugar with the vanilla essence in a bowl until light and fluffy. Add the lightly whisked eggs and ground hazelnuts alternately. Beat well. Stir in the candied peel and shelled walnuts thoroughly. Sift the flour, salt and baking powder together on to the mixture and lightly fold in with a metal spoon. Turn the mixture into the cake tin and smooth the top. Bake in the centre of the oven for 50–60 minutes until firm and springy to a light touch in the centre. Cool in the tin before turning out, and if necessary loosen the sides with a knife. Melt the redcurrant jelly in a pan and use it to glaze the cake all over with a pastry brush. Then sprinkle demerara sugar (if you have any of that crystallised preserving sugar it looks prettier and is wonderfully crunchy) all over the top and sides of the cake and decorate with whole hazelnuts and walnuts. Serve with cream.

Gâteau Africaine

This is perhaps my favourite chocolate cake. It's damp, rich and gooey, much more of a pudding than a cake. Iced with fresh cream and trickled with strands of melted chocolate, it is irresistible even to the most strong-minded slimmer.

4 oz plus 1 oz plain chocolate (110 g plus 25 g)
5 tablespoonfuls water
6 oz butter or margarine (110 g)
5 oz soft brown sugar (150 g)
3 large eggs – separated
2 oz ground almonds (50 g)
2 oz fresh white breadcrumbs (50 g)
1 heaped teaspoonful ground cinnamon
apricot jam
¼ pint double or whipping cream (150 ml)

Grease a fairly shallow 8 in (20 cm) cake tin and line with a disc of greased greaseproof paper. Heat the oven to Gas Mark 5/375°F. Melt 4 oz (110 g) of the chocolate with the water and stir until smooth. Leave to cool slightly. Beat the butter until soft, add the brown sugar and beat until fluffy. Beat in the egg yolks, followed by the ground almonds and the melted chocolate. Stir in the bread-crumbs and cinnamon. Whisk the egg whites until they stand in soft peaks. Then, using a metal spoon, fold them gently into the chocolate mixture and spoon evenly into the prepared cake tin. Bake in the centre of the oven for 40–50 minutes until springy to a touch in the centre. Cool in the tin. Then loosen the edges with a knife and turn out.

Melt the remaining 1 oz (25 g) of chocolate with 1 tablespoonful of water, stir until smooth and leave to cool. Put the cake on to a serving plate and spread all over with apricot jam. Whisk the cream until thick and ice first the sides and then the top of the cake with it in rough flicks. Then, holding the spoon high above the cake, trickle the cooled chocolate over the cake in a thin criss-cross pattern. Leave in a very cool place, preferably not in the fridge, until ready to serve.

Chocolate Torte with Apricot Sauce

A moist, chocolate-speckled cake which you can either ice as a normal cake or serve this way as a pudding with hot apricot sauce and, if you like, with cream too.

5 oz soft margarine (150 g)
5 oz castor sugar (150 g)
1 teaspoonful vanilla essence
4 eggs – separated
5 oz plain chocolate – grated (150 g)
3 oz self-raising flour (75 g)
3–4 tablespoonfuls apricot jam
juice of 1 lemon
sprinkling of icing sugar

Pre-heat the oven to Gas Mark 4/350°F and put a disc of greased greaseproof paper in the bottom of a 6–7 in (15–18 cm) cake tin. Cream the margarine with the sugar and vanilla essence. Beat in the egg yolks thoroughly. Stir in the grated chocolate well and then sift in the flour. Stir that in with a metal spoon. Whisk the egg whites until stiff and stir in with a metal spoon. Put into the cake tin and bake in the centre of the oven for 60–70 minutes until a sharp knife inserted in the middle comes out clean. Take out and leave in the tin for 10 minutes before loosening the sides with a knife and turning out. Cool on a wire rack. Transfer to a serving plate and sprinkle the top with icing sugar through a sieve. Heat the jam with the lemon juice in a saucepan and, if it is very lumpy, put through a sieve and re-heat if necessary.

Fruity Chocolate Crunch

If you are looking for something quick and foolproof to make, this is for you. Simply mixing the ingredients and chilling in the fridge produces a sophisticated dessert cake.

FOR THE CAKE
4 oz butter or margarine (110 g)
2 tablespoonfuls golden syrup
5 oz plain chocolate (150 g)
8 oz plain sweet biscuits – crushed (225 g)
3 oz glacé cherries – roughly chopped (75 g)
2 oz raisins (50 g)
2 oz chopped candied peel (50 g)
1 rounded teaspoonful ground cinnamon

FOR THE ICING (optional)
2 heaped tablespoonfuls icing sugar
2 teaspoonfuls warm water
1 or 2 glacé cherries

Lightly oil a small loaf or cake tin (1-pint/½-litre capacity). Gently melt the butter, golden syrup and chocolate in a saucepan. When smooth, stir in the rest of the ingredients. Spoon the mixture into the prepared tin and smooth the top. Cool and then chill in the fridge. To turn out dip the tin in hot water for a moment and then plop the cake on to a serving dish. To ice, stir the icing sugar and water together until smooth and then spread over the top of the cake, letting it dribble down the sides. Decorate with halved or chopped glacé cherries. Chill again in the fridge. When serving cut into thin slices and eat with or without cream. It's specially good with vanilla ice cream.

Mrs. Edmonds' Orange Chocolate Cake

Mrs Edmonds was a history teacher at an English girls' boarding school. She became particularly popular with her pupils because of the irresistible chocolate cake she made for the lucky ones who came to tea with her. It is simple to make and perfect as a pudding cake served with cream. It may make you as popular as Mrs. Edmonds!

FOR THE CAKE
4 oz butter or margarine (110 g)
4 oz castor sugar (110 g)
grated rind of 1 orange and 1 lemon
2 oz drinking chocolate powder (50 g)
4 oz ground almonds (110 g)

2 large eggs – lightly beaten
1 tablespoonful brandy, rum or orange juice
2 oz self-raising flour (50 g)
1 heaped tablespoonful dark marmalade

FOR THE ICING
4 oz plain chocolate (110 g)
1 oz butter or margarine (25 g)

Heat the oven to Gas Mark 3/325°F. Grease a 7 in (18 cm) cake tin and line with a disc of greased greaseproof paper. Lightly flour the tin. Cream the butter and sugar until fluffy. Beat in the orange and lemon rind. Stir in the chocolate powder and ground almonds and beat until well mixed. Then add the eggs with a teaspoonful of flour and the alcohol or orange juice and beat or whisk thoroughly. Sift in the remaining flour and fold into the mixture with a metal spoon. Transfer to the prepared tin and bake in the centre of the oven for 40–50 minutes until springy to touch in the centre. Put on a rack to cool.

When cold, melt the marmalade slightly in a pan and brush the cake all over with it. Now break up the chocolate, and melt with one teaspoonful of water in a double boiler or a bowl over a pan of hot water. Stir until smooth and then stir in the butter or margarine. Cool until it is of spreading consistency and then coat the cake with the chocolate. If you have any, decorate with a little extra grated or thinly pared orange rind. Let the chocolate set and serve with cream.

PARTY PIECES

Marmalade Soufflé

I hate a last-minute panic when I am cooking a meal for several people, so I nearly always choose a pudding which can be prepared beforehand. However, a beautifully risen, steaming hot soufflé is such a treat and as long as you can get your guests to eat it at the right moment, it is simple to do. The easiest way is to prepare the main mixture beforehand, then you will only have to fold in the whisked egg whites just before you put the soufflé in the oven. Even if the soufflé is ready before you have finished the first course it will stay risen for a bit if you turn off the heat and leave it in the oven without opening the oven door.

2 oz butter (50 g)
1½ oz plain flour (40 g)
½ pint milk (275 ml)
2 heaped tablespoonfuls marmalade
1 dessertspoon golden syrup or honey
4 eggs – separated
pinch of cream of tartar
1 oz plain chocolate – grated (25 g)

Gently melt the butter in a pan. Remove from the heat and stir in the flour. Gradually stir in the milk. Bring to the boil stirring all the time and let it bubble, still stirring, for 2 minutes. Remove from the heat and stir in the marmalade and the golden syrup until dissolved and blended in. Heat the oven to Gas Mark 5/375°F. Butter a 2½-pint (1½-litre) soufflé dish or other round ovenproof dish. Then add the egg yolks to the mixture and stir in. Finally, whisk the egg whites with the cream of tartar until they stand in peaks and, using a metal spoon, fold lightly into the yolk mixture. Pour into the prepared dish and sprinkle with the grated chocolate. Cook in the centre of the oven for 40–45 minutes until well risen and dark brown on top. Serve at once with cream.

Chilled Melon and Walnut Soufflé

The delicate flavour of the melon is brought out by the sharp lemon custard in this light and refreshing pudding.

2 large lemons (or 3 smaller ones)
3 eggs – separated
3 oz castor sugar (75 g)
1 packet or ½ oz gelatine (10 g)
2 oz chopped walnuts plus a few
extra for garnish (50 g)
1 melon – 1¾–2¼ lb (800 g–1 kg)

Grate the rind of the lemons and put in a basin with the egg yolks and sugar. Gradually stir in the lemon juice and put the basin over a pan of gently simmering water for about 5 minutes, stirring constantly until the mixture thickens to the consistency of a medium thick sauce. Dissolve the gelatine in 4 tablespoonfuls of very hot water and stir into the lemon yolk mixture. Allow to cool. Then cut the peel off the melon, slice up into smallish pieces and stir into the cooled yolk mixture with the walnuts. Whisk the egg whites until thick and fold into the mixture lightly but thoroughly. Transfer to a serving bowl and chill until set. Then arrange a few walnut halves or pieces on top and serve with cream.

Caramel Soufflé in a Pond

If you like the flavour of crème caramel this is a rather more luxurious way of producing it. The nuts, enveloped in the light mixture, make an interesting texture.

1 oz gelatine (25 g)
4 tablespoonfuls hot water
4 large egg yolks
8 oz granulated sugar (225 g)
4 tablespoonfuls water
¼ pint hot water (275 ml)
2 oz chopped nuts (50 g) – hazelnuts,
almonds or walnuts
4 large egg whites
¼ pint single cream (150 ml)

Dissolve the gelatine in a cup with 4 tablespoonfuls of hot water and set the cup in a bowl of hot water to keep the gelatine liquid (this will also help it to dissolve smoothly). Whisk the egg yolks until paler in colour and slightly thicker. Dissolve the sugar in another 4 tablespoonfuls of water over a low heat. Then increase the heat and boil fiercely, without stirring, until the caramel is light golden brown – 2–4 minutes. Don't let it get too brown or the soufflé will taste burnt. Remove from the heat and allow the bubbles to subside. Then gradually stir in ½ pint (150 ml) of hot water. Again return to a low heat and stir to make sure all the caramel is dissolved. Remove from the heat and stir in the dissolved gelatine, then pour the caramel liquid mixture gradually on to the egg yolks in a thin stream, whisking all the time.

Lightly oil a 2-pint (1-litre) soufflé dish. Let the yolk and caramel mixture cool until just beginning to set. Then stir in all but a heaped teaspoonful of the chopped nuts. Lastly, whisk the egg whites until stiff and fold into the caramel mixture. Pour into the oiled dish and chill well until set. To turn out dip the dish briefly in hot water, then put the dish upside down on to a large serving plate and shake out. Sprinkle the reserved nuts on top and pour the cream round the edge of the soufflé.

Black Treacle Soufflé

Some people have a passion for the strong taste of black treacle. If you don't you can make this creamy cold soufflé with honey, using lemon juice instead of orange, or alternatively, with golden syrup, adding a teaspoonful of ground cinnamon.

3 large eggs
2 rounded tablespoonfuls black treacle
juice of ½ orange
¼ pint double cream (150 ml)
pinch of cream of tartar or salt
chopped hazelnuts or walnuts to decorate

Put the egg yolks in a deep bowl and put the whites aside in another bowl. Add the treacle and orange juice to the yolks and put the bowl over a pan of very hot, not boiling, water. Whisk until thick and pale brown. (This will be much quicker – 5–8 minutes – and no effort if you have an electric hand whisk.) Remove the bowl from the pan. Whip the cream until thick but not stiff and stir lightly into the treacle mixture. Whisk the egg whites with the cream of tartar or salt until they stand in peaks. Fold into the treacle mixture and transfer to a serving bowl. Chill in the fridge and serve the same day, sprinkled with chopped nuts and accompanied by thin sweet biscuits.

Signorina Salvini's Chocolate Dolce

This is like a crunchy, gooey chocolate mousse. It is irresistible but take care, as it is very rich. I find it best to serve it in little individual dishes to curb over-indulgence!

3 oz plain chocolate (75 g)
6 oz butter (175 g)
3 eggs – separated
4 oz castor sugar (110 g)
5 oz plain biscuits – roughly
crushed (150 g)
$\frac{1}{4}$ -pint double or whipping cream (150 ml)
1 square of plain chocolate – grated

Melt the chocolate and butter in a bowl over a pan of hot water. Beat the yolks and sugar together until pale. Stir in the crushed biscuits and gradually stir in the melted chocolate and butter. Mix well together. If the mixture seems very warm, cool slightly. Whisk the whites of eggs until stiff and fold gently into the chocolate mixture with a metal spoon. Put into a serving bowl or into little dishes and chill in the fridge for at least 8 hours or overnight. Then whip the cream until stiff, spread on top of the chocolate mixture and sprinkle with grated chocolate. Keep in the fridge until ready to serve.

BOP—5

Cranberry and Orange Mould

Here is a sharp and refreshing mousse-like pudding to have after a rich meal. Although it is made with cranberries which we only seem to find in the shops in mid-winter, it has a summery taste which will lighten a dark winter's day.

6 oz fresh cranberries (175 g)
juice of 4 oranges and 1 lemon
5 oz granulated sugar (150 g)
½ oz or 1 packet gelatine (10 g)
2 large eggs – separated
¼ pint double or whipping cream (150 ml)
½–1 oz chopped roasted nuts (10–25 g)

Put the cranberries, orange and lemon juice into a pan, bring to the boil and simmer for 7–8 minutes. Add the sugar and gelatine and stir over a gentle heat until dissolved. Put the egg yolks into a bowl and gradually pour the hot cranberries and orange juice on to them, stirring all the time. Leave to cool but not set. Whisk the cream until softly thick and stir into the cranberry mixture. Then whisk the egg whites until stiff and fold them gently in. Pour into a ring mould or a round dish and leave to set in the fridge. When well set dip the mould briefly in very hot water and then shake out on to a serving plate. Sprinkle chopped nuts all over the pudding, pressing them on to the sides as well. Chill again before serving.

Ginger and Orange Snowball

One rainy afternoon I sat in my kitchen, totally uninspired, trying to think of original puddings for this book. I looked in my cupboard for ingredients and could only see a dreary looking packet of trifle sponges. "Oh well," I thought, "today I'll just have to make something ordinary which will do for the children." In fact what turned out was the most mouth watering concoction of which the children had only the remains after a group of adults had enthusiastically eaten most of it at dinner that evening.

8 oz full cream cheese (225 g)
3 oz castor sugar (75 g)
3 oz unsalted butter – melted (75 g)
2 oz chopped hazelnuts (50 g)
1 oz candied peel (25 g)
2 oz crystallised ginger – chopped,
plus a little for decoration (50 g)
grated rind and juice of 2 medium
oranges and 1 lemon
8 trifle sponges
$\frac{1}{2}$ oz or 1 packet gelatine (10 g)
$\frac{1}{4}$ pint double or whipping cream (150 ml)

Beat the cream cheese with the sugar and the melted butter until smooth and creamy. Stir in the chopped nuts, candied peel and chopped ginger and the grated rind of the oranges and the lemon. Slice the trifle sponges into 2 or 3 thin slices each. Put 3 or 4 slices on the bottom of a 2-pint (1-litre) pudding basin. Then spoon on a layer of the cream cheese mixture, then another layer of sponges and so on, ending with a layer of sponges.

Make the juice of the oranges and lemon up to $\frac{3}{4}$ pint (425 ml) with hot water. Dissolve the gelatine in a cup with 2 tablespoonfuls of very hot water and stir into the juices. Strain the juice over the mixture in the pudding basin, making sure the juice seeps to the bottom of the basin by pulling the mixture back with a spoon. Put in the fridge to set. When well chilled dip the basin briefly in hot water and turn out on to a serving plate. Whisk the cream until thick and ice the pudding all over with it. Decorate the top with a little chopped ginger and chill again in the fridge before serving.

Stuffed Peaches

When my husband tried this pudding he said, "This is the kind of food which soldiers at the front dreamed about!" It certainly looks and tastes particularly luscious; moist fresh peaches swimming in a sharp redcurrant sauce and stuffed to overflowing with a nutty mixture of cream cheese and whipped cream.

2 tablespoonfuls redcurrant jelly
grated rind and juice of 1 lemon
6 ripe peaches
4 oz cream cheese (110 g)
2 oz castor sugar (50 g)
¼ pint double or whipping cream (150 ml)
1 oz chopped hazelnuts, almonds
or walnuts (25 g)
1 tablespoonful demerara sugar

Grate the lemon rind and put on one side. Put the redcurrant jelly into a pan and melt gently. Add all but three teaspoonfuls of the lemon juice and stir until smooth. Pour the redcurrant sauce on to a flat serving dish. Put the peaches in a bowl and pour boiling water over them, leave for 30 seconds, then remove the peaches and peel off the skins. Cut them in half, remove the stones and arrange the halves on the plate of redcurrant sauce, hollow side uppermost. Beat the cream cheese with the castor sugar until soft and fluffy. Beat in the reserved 3 teaspoonfuls of lemon juice. Whisk the cream until thick and stir it into the cream cheese mixture. Stir in the reserved lemon rind and the chopped nuts. Pile this mixture on to the peach halves and sprinkle the demerara sugar on top. Chill until ready to serve.

Delice de Petit Suisse

The most luscious dessert, and quick to make too. It's the mildest light and creamy cheese cake coated in roasted almonds and topped with a purée of scarlet cranberries. Cranberries are of course good for the winter but in season you could use a thick blackcurrant or damson purée instead. In midsummer fresh strawberries or raspberries piled on top and then coated thickly with icing sugar at the last moment are delicious. If you can't get the Petit Suisse cheeses, which have a particularly creamy taste and texture, use any other full cream cheese.

6 oz fresh cranberries (175 g)
5 tablespoonfuls water
4 oz granulated sugar (110 g)
1 oz flaked almonds (25 g)
8–10 fl oz double cream (225–275 ml)
2 heaped tablespoonfuls icing sugar
6 Petit Suisse cream cheeses

Put the cranberries and water in a pan, cover and bring to the boil. Simmer gently for 8–10 minutes until all the cranberries have popped. Remove from the heat, add the granulated sugar and stir until dissolved. Cool slightly and then whizz in a liquidiser until smooth. Chill the purée in the fridge.

Meanwhile put the almond flakes on a baking sheet in a medium oven until just golden brown – 5–10 minutes. Leave to cool. Beat the Petit Suisse cheese until soft. Whisk the cream until stiff, stir in the icing sugar and then fold thoroughly into the Petit Suisse cheeses. Pile the mixture into the middle of a circular serving plate and then, using a wide knife or spatula, shape and smooth into a cake shape about 6 in (15 cm) in diameter. Chill in the fridge for at least 1 hour. Shortly before serving press about half the roasted almonds round the sides of the cake. Spoon the chilled cranberry purée on the top and sprinkle with the rest of the nuts. Chill until ready to serve. Best eaten the day it is made.

Raspberries in a Creamy Blanket

While the flavour of strawberries is brought out by lemon or orange juice, raspberries are best simply with cream. This way of serving them wrapped in a rich mixture of cream cheese and soured cream makes even rather small or over-ripe raspberries most luscious.

4 oz cream cheese (110 g)
2–3 oz castor sugar – to taste (50–75 g)
1 carton soured cream
1 lb raspberries (450 g)
1 oz chopped nuts (25 g)

Beat the cream cheese and sugar until soft and fluffy and beat in the soured cream. Then gently fold in the raspberries and spoon the mixture into a serving bowl. Chill for an hour or two in the fridge. Before serving sprinkle the chopped nuts on top.

Strawberries in Orange Cream

A mouthwatering way to serve strawberries and especially useful if you haven't got quite enough to go round. The orange juice enhances the flavour of the fruit and the slightly sharp-tasting cream is delicious. When strawberries are over you can use raspberries, loganberries and later blackberries.

1 lb strawberries (450 g)
8–10 fl oz double cream or
whipping cream (225–275 ml)
2–3 tablespoonfuls castor sugar
1 small carton plain yoghurt
grated rind and juice of 1 small orange

Take the stalks off the strawberries and halve them if they are large. In a large bowl whip the cream until thick and then stir in the sugar, the yoghurt, the grated orange rind and then gradually the orange juice. Lightly stir in the strawberries and transfer the mixture to a pretty glass bowl if possible. Chill in the fridge before serving.

Lemon Fluff Julius

Julius has been cook in a private house outside Cape Town for thirty years and his food is magical. When we had dinner there everyone, even the slimmers, had at least two helpings of this creation, which is a golden featherlight froth of sharpest lemon on a crumbly shortbread base. It is best eaten hot and well risen, though it will only sink a little if it is more convenient to eat it cold. I always make the first two stages, the base and the lemon custard, well in advance, so that it is only a question of whisking and folding in the egg whites just before cooking.

FOR THE SHORTBREAD BASE
6 oz plain flour (175 g)
½ teaspoonful salt
1 rounded tablespoonful castor sugar
5 oz soft butter (150 g)

FOR THE FLUFF
grated rind of 2 lemons
¼ pint lemon juice – 3–4 lemons according to size (150 ml)
4 large eggs – separated
3 oz castor sugar (75 g)
pinch of salt

Butter a rather shallow 9 in (23 cm) flan dish. Sift the flour, salt and sugar for the shortbread into a bowl. Work the butter into the flour with your fingertips. Using floured hands, as it will be rather sticky, gather the mixture together and press it lightly but evenly down over the bottom of the flan dish. Prick all over with a fork and if there is time, leave in the fridge for about 30 minutes. Heat the oven to Gas Mark 6/400°F and cook the shortbread in the centre of the oven for about 15 to 20 minutes until light brown. Cool.

While the shortbread is cooking you can begin to make the lemon fluff. Grate the rind of 2 lemons and put on one side. Now squeeze the juice from 3–4 lemons to make ¼ pint (150 ml). Put the yolks of the eggs into the top of a double boiler or into a pudding basin which will fit over a pan of water. Stir in the sugar and then the lemon juice a little at a time. Put the pan or basin over gently simmering water and cook to make a custard, stirring all the time with a wooden spoon, until it is thick enough to coat the spoon. Stir in the grated rind and leave to cool. If you want to continue immediately you only need cool the custard slightly, otherwise you can leave it all until you are ready to cook the pudding.

Reduce the oven heat to Gas Mark 2/300°F. Add a pinch of salt to the egg whites and whisk until stiff. Using a metal spoon, lightly fold the cooled lemon custard into the egg whites. Pile the mixture on top of the shortbread base and cook towards the top of the oven for 50–60 minutes until dark golden brown. Serve immediately with or without cream.

N.B. Julius served this with a bowl of fresh mulberries from the garden, well sprinkled with sugar – raspberries are equally delicious with it.

Chocolate and Raisin Cheesecake

This unusual cheesecake has a crunchy shortbread base with a dark chocolate and raisin topping and is popular with the children.

FOR THE SHORTBREAD BASE
4 oz plain flour (110 g)
2 oz castor sugar (50 g)
2 oz fine semolina (50 g)
4 oz butter or margarine – at room temperature (110 g)

FOR THE CHEESECAKE
4 oz cream cheese (110 g)
2 oz castor sugar (50 g)
1 small carton yoghurt
1 egg – lightly whisked

FOR THE TOPPING
2 oz plain chocolate (50 g)
2 oz soft dark brown sugar (50 g)
3 tablespoonfuls water
1 oz butter (25 g)
2 oz raisins (50 g)

Heat the oven to Gas Mark 2/300°F. Butter a round china or earthenware 7–8 in (18–20 cm) flan dish. Warm a mixing bowl and put into it the flour, sugar and semolina. Work the butter in with your fingers until thoroughly blended. Gather up into a ball of dough. Press the dough evenly over the bottom of the flan dish. Prick all over with a fork and bake in the centre of the oven for 15 minutes.

Meanwhile, beat or whisk up the cream cheese with 2 oz (50 g) castor sugar and the yoghurt until smooth. Whisk in the egg. Pour the mixture into the flan case on top of the shortbread. Return to the oven for another 45 minutes.

To make the topping, put the chocolate, water and brown sugar in a bowl over a pan of very hot water and stir until smooth. Add the butter and stir until dissolved. Stir in the raisins. Smooth the mixture on top of the flan. Leave to get cold in a cool place but not in the fridge. This flan is very rich and needs no cream.

Ginger and Lemon Cheesecake

This is the kind of cheesecake which you don't have to cook. It's light but creamy and the mixture of the ginger and lemon is mouthwatering.

FOR THE BISCUIT BASE
4 oz ginger biscuits (110 g)
1 oz butter (25 g)
1 tablespoonful sugar

FOR THE FILLING
8 oz full cream cheese (225 g)
4 oz castor sugar (110 g)
3 eggs – separated
grated rind and juice of 1 large lemon
½ oz or 1 packet gelatine (10 g)
2 oz crystallised ginger – chopped finely (50 g)
pinch of salt
1 oz chopped nuts or extra chopped ginger (25 g)

Crush the ginger biscuits under a rolling pin or in a liquidiser. Melt the butter with the tablespoonful of sugar and stir in the crushed biscuits. Lightly oil an 8 in (20 cm) loose-bottomed cake tin. Press the biscuit mixture on to the bottom and smooth with a metal spoon. Beat the cream cheese with the castor sugar and egg yolks until smooth. Put the grated lemon rind on one side. Warm the juice in a pan with 2 tablespoonfuls of water and dissolve the gelatine in it. Beat or whisk thoroughly into the cream cheese mixture and stir in the lemon rind and the crystallised ginger. Add the salt to the egg whites and whisk until thick but don't let them break up. Fold gently into the cheese mixture and pour into the cake tin. Chill in the fridge until set and then sprinkle some chopped nuts on top. Press the cheesecake up out of the cake tin and put on to a serving dish.

Orange and Raspberry Roulade

This is a perfect light and moist pudding, especially delicious in summer when you can use fresh raspberries (or strawberries) which ooze out with the cream. But it is also well worth making in winter, using good raspberry or strawberry jam.

5 eggs – separated
5 oz castor sugar (150 g)
4 oz ground almonds (110 g)
1 level teaspoonful baking powder
grated rind and juice of 1 small orange
¼ teaspoonful cream of tartar
about ¾ lb fresh raspberries or ½ pot
of raspberry jam (350 g)
½ pint double or whipping cream (275 ml)
icing sugar

Heat the oven to Gas Mark 4/350°F. Lightly oil a Swiss roll tin measuring approximately 14 × 10 in (35.5 × 25.5 cm). Line the bottom with a piece of greaseproof paper, also lightly oiled. Whisk the yolks of the eggs with about three quarters of the castor sugar until pale and thick, not stiff. Stir in the ground almonds, baking powder and the grated orange rind. Gradually stir in the orange juice. Whisk the egg whites with the cream of tartar until stiff and then whisk in the remaining castor sugar a little at a time. Using a metal spoon, fold the whites gently into the yolk mixture. Pour the mixture into the prepared tin and smooth evenly. Cook in the centre of the oven for 20–25 minutes until springy in the centre.

Allow to cool – it will sink a bit but this doesn't matter. When cool cover with a sheet of greaseproof paper and a cloth and leave in the fridge for 2–3 hours or overnight if possible. To turn out, loosen the edges with a knife. Sprinkle a sheet of greaseproof paper with sieved icing sugar and turn the roulade out on to it. If using fresh raspberries, whip the cream until stiff and stir the raspberries into it. Spread the mixture over the roulade. If using jam, spread the jam on first, then the whipped cream. With the help of the greaseproof paper, roll up gently and rather loosely. Unless you are very lucky, the roll is almost certain to crack a little as the mixture is so light. Don't worry, this makes it look it more irresistible!

Pâtisserie Bouffante

Your friends may well imagine, when you present them with this featherlight tower of puffed up pastry layers, that you bought it from some expensive French pâtisserie. And as it crumbles and melts in their mouths they will never guess it not only cost you very little but was a minimum of trouble to make. The extra puffed-up crisp but melting pastry is achieved by frying the layers instead of baking them, and they are sandwiched together with oozing jam and crunchy roasted almond flakes. In the summer you can alter the filling. Try black cherry jam with fresh red currants, or a sharp crab apple jelly with raspberries, or simply whipped cream and strawberries – quite delicious!

2 oz flaked almonds (50 g)
8 oz packet puff pastry (225 g)
sunflower or groundnut oil to fry in
about $\frac{1}{2}$ jar apricot jam
1–2 tablespoonfuls icing sugar

Spread the flaked almonds on a baking sheet and put into a medium to high oven for a few minutes until crisp and golden brown. Cut the pastry into six pieces. Form into balls and roll out very thinly on a lightly floured board into six circles about 8–9 in (20–23 cm) diameter. Some will probably be a little bigger than others, some more of a real circle, too – it doesn't matter.

Cover the bottom of a large frying pan with about $\frac{1}{4}$ in ($\frac{1}{2}$ cm) of sunflower oil. Make it very hot and, one by one, fry the pastry circles on each side just until golden brown. They will cook very quickly so don't leave the stove. Drain on absorbent paper. Then put one circle on a serving plate and spread it lightly (so as not to crush the tender pastry) with some jam. Then sprinkle over some roasted almond flakes. Put another pastry circle on top and continue like this in layers, spreading jam and sprinkling with almond flakes. When you put on the last circle sprinkle icing sugar through a fine sieve quite thickly all over the top and scatter the last few almonds in the centre. If you are not going to eat it at once, it will keep all right for at least a day. Keep it in a fairly airy place, but don't put it in the fridge. To serve, cut in slices with a sharp knife. It can be accompanied by cream if you like but, personally, I think it is better without.

Hazelnut Meringue Cake with Brandy Chocolate Filling

Two lovely nutty meringue cakes sandwiched together with a rich chocolate custard, made with the egg yolks.

FOR THE CAKE
4 large egg whites
pinch of salt
8 oz castor sugar (225 g)
1 teaspoonful vanilla essence
1 teaspoonful vinegar
2 oz ground hazelnuts (50 g) —
you can buy these ready ground in
health food shops but otherwise a
liquidiser will grind whole nuts
within seconds

FOR THE FILLING
4 large egg yolks
½ teaspoonful cornflour
1 oz castor sugar (25 g)
1 tablespoonful or a little
more of brandy
¼ pint milk (150 ml)
2 oz plain chocolate—coarsely
grated (50 g)

Grease two 8 in (20 cm) sandwich tins with a disc of greased greaseproof paper. Pre-heat the oven to Gas Mark 4/350°F. Whisk the egg whites with the salt until stiff and then add the sugar a little at a time and whisk until the mixture stands in peaks. With a metal spoon lightly stir in the vanilla essence, the vinegar and ground nuts. Divide the mixture between the two tins and bake in the centre of the oven for 30–40 minutes until firm to touch. While the cakes are cooking you can prepare the filling. When cooked cool the cakes slightly in the tins, ease the edges with a sharp knife and cool on a wire rack.

To make the filling, put the yolks in the top of a double boiler or in a bowl over a pan of hot water with the cornflour, sugar and the brandy and mix up together. Stir in the milk. Put over a pan of simmering water and cook until the mixture has become thick, stirring all the time with a wooden spoon. Then stir in the chocolate until melted and smooth. Remove from the heat and transfer to a bowl to cool. When cool, spread the chocolate custard in between the two meringue cakes. Chill in the fridge before serving.

Flaky Summer Sandwich

This is a mouthwatering pudding, the kind which everyone loves. It's a festive-looking gâteau of cream and summer fruits sandwiched between crisp, flaky, orange-flavoured pastry and is far simpler to make than anyone would think.

FOR THE PASTRY
8 oz strong plain flour (225 g)
½ teaspoonful salt
grated rind and juice of 1 orange
6 oz (175 g) from an 8 oz (225 g)
block of frozen butter or margarine
3 tablespoonfuls very cold water

FOR THE FILLING
6–8 fl oz double cream
(175–225 ml)
½–¾ lb fresh soft summer fruit –
strawberries, raspberries, stoned
cherries, sliced peaches, etc.
(225–350 g)
a little castor sugar
1–2 teaspoonfuls icing sugar

Sift the flour and salt into a bowl. Add the orange rind. Put a grater into the bowl on top of the flour. Hold the frozen block of butter at one end with its wrapping and coarsely grate off three quarters of the block. Using a round-bladed knife mix the fat roughly into the flour until crumbly. Now add the orange juice and the cold water, mixing again with the knife. Gather up the dough in your hands and press into a ball. Wrap up in foil or plastic and refrigerate for at least 1 hour.

Heat the oven to Gas Mark 7/524°F. Butter 2 × 8–9 in (20–23 cm) sandwich tins. Then cut the pastry in half and shape each half into a ball. Roll out into two rather thick circles, big enough to fit tightly into the sandwich tins. If necessary, press over the edges to neaten. Prick all over with a fork and bake just above the centre of the oven for 20–25 minutes until risen and golden brown. Take out and cool in the tins. Then put one pastry round on to a serving plate. Whisk the cream until thick and spread half of it on to the pastry round. Then pile on a thick layer of soft fruit, sprinkled with a little castor sugar, and then the other half of the cream dolloped on. Top with the other pastry round. Sprinkle the icing sugar through a fine sieve over the top of the gâteau. Leave in a cool dry place until needed but not in the fridge as this would make the pastry less crisp.

Angel's Cloud Cake

This is truly a fantasy pudding, looking quite unreal and beautiful. The lightest bright white cake is sandwiched together with a fresh lemon curd made from the egg yolks. It is one of those puddings which will make people gasp!

FOR THE CAKE
1½ oz self-raising flour (40 g)
½ oz cornflour (10 g)
5 oz castor sugar (150 g)
4 large egg whites
1 tablespoonful cold water
½ teaspoonful cream of tartar
pinch of salt
1 teaspoonful lemon essence

FOR THE FILLING AND ICING
4 egg yolks
grated rind and juice of 2 lemons
3 oz castor sugar (75 g)
8 fl oz double or whipping cream
(225 ml)

Have ready an ungreased 7½ – 8 in (19–20 cm) deep cake tin lined with a disc of greaseproof paper. Heat the oven to Gas Mark 1/275°F. It is important that the flour should be very fine, so sift both flours through a very fine sieve several times. Then sift the castor sugar and add 1 heaped tablespoonful of it to the sifted flour. Put the egg whites into a large bowl with the water and cream of tartar and salt and whisk until they stand in soft peaks. Using a metal spoon lightly fold in the sugar, a tablespoonful at a time, and add the essence. Lastly, fold in the sifted flours, sifting them once more on to the egg whites, a teaspoonful at a time. Pour the mixture into the cake tin and bake on a low shelf in the oven for 1¼–1½ hours until well risen and springy to a light touch in the centre.

While the cake is cooking make the lemon filling. Put the egg yolks into the top of a double boiler or into a bowl which you can set over a pan of water. Stir in the sugar and grate in the lemon rind. Then squeeze out the lemon juice and stir it into the yolks gradually. Cook over gently simmering water, stirring all the time with a wooden spoon until it is thick enough to coat the back of the spoon. Leave to get completely cold.

When the cake has cooked leave it in the tin until cold, then loosen the sides with a knife and turn out, removing the disc of greaseproof paper. Using a very sharp knife cut the cake carefully in half, put one half on a serving plate and spread on the lemon filling. Top with the other half of the cake. Whip the cream until very thick and spread roughly all over the top and sides of the cake with a knife. Chill in the fridge before serving.

Angel's Almond Cloud Cake

An almond-flavoured version of this lightest and most dreamy pudding. Instead of being sandwiched together with a filling it has a lovely topping of honeyed egg custard and crunchy chopped almonds.

FOR THE CAKE
Ingredients as in previous recipe for Angel's Cloud Cake but using ¼ teaspoon almond essence instead of lemon.

FOR THE TOPPING
4 egg yolks
1 level tablespoonful honey
6 tablespoonfuls milk
¼ teaspoonful almond essence
5–6 fl oz double cream
(150–175 ml)
2 oz unblanched almonds – roughly chopped (50 g)

Make the cake as in the previous recipe, using almond essence instead of lemon. While the cake is cooking make the filling. As in the previous recipe put the egg yolks in the top of a double boiler or basin set over a pan of water. Stir in the honey, milk and essence. Cook, stirring all the time with a wooden spoon, over gently simmering water until the custard coats the back of the spoon. Cool completely. When the cake is cold loosen the edges with a knife and turn out on to a serving plate. Spread the cold custard on top. Whip the cream until thick and cover the sides of the cake with it. Lastly sprinkle the chopped almonds all over the custard.

Rum Savarin (serves 8–10)

This version of a succulent French savarin is successfully made without yeast. It will feed a large number of people and, being made in advance, is particularly useful for a party. To fill the centre of the rum and syrup soaked ring a good imitation of the slightly sharp Crème Fraîche used in France is made by adding a little plain yoghurt to whipped cream. You can also mix this with stewed fruit if you like, and of course during the summer with fresh cherries and other soft fruits.

FOR THE SAVARIN
2 oz butter and a little more (50 g)
3 large eggs – separated
3 oz castor sugar (75 g)
4 tablespoonfuls milk (at room temperature)
6 oz self-raising flour (175 g)

FOR THE SYRUP
8 oz granulated sugar (225 g)
1 small wineglass of dark rum
1 small wineglass of water

FOR THE CRÈME FRAÎCHE
6–8 fl oz double or whipping cream (175–225 ml)
1–1½ tablespoonfuls plain yoghurt

First generously butter and dust with flour a savarin mould or ring mould tin – 2-pint (1-litre) capacity. Heat the oven to Gas Mark 5/375°F. Melt the butter in a pan and put on one side. Whisk the egg yolks with the castor sugar and milk until pale and frothy. Sift the flour into a bowl and, using a metal spoon, gently stir into the mixture followed by the warm melted butter. Finally whisk the egg whites until stiff and fold them carefully into the batter. Spread evenly into the prepared savarin mould and bake in the centre of the oven for 25–35 minutes until well risen and golden brown.

Now make the syrup. Dissolve the granulated sugar with the rum and water over a low heat, then bring to the boil and boil fiercely for 2–3 minutes. Meanwhile turn out the cake on to a fairly large plate. Prick all over and right through with a thin skewer. Pour the boiling syrup evenly over the warm cake and leave to soak it up for several hours or overnight. Then, shortly before serving, spread the cold syrup which has dripped on to the plate over the savarin. Whisk the cream until stiff and then stir the yoghurt into it and spoon into the centre of the savarin ring.

Chocolate Floating Island

There seem to be so many versions of either the English Floating Island pudding or the French Iles Flottantes. Here is my version of a chocolate-topped pudding, easy to make, with a consistency which not only melts but literally vanishes in your mouth. Floating in a sea of brandied custard sauce, it could hardly be more delicious.

2 oz plain chocolate (50 g)
1 level tablespoonful honey or
golden syrup
1 tablespoonful water
4 eggs – separated
2 oz plus 1 level tablespoonful
castor sugar (50 g)
1 tablespoonful brandy
$\frac{1}{4}$ pint double or single cream (150 ml)

Gently melt the chocolate in a saucepan with the honey and water and stir until smooth. Pour into the bottom of a 2–2$\frac{1}{2}$-pint (1–1$\frac{1}{2}$-litre) soufflé dish. Whisk the egg whites until thick and then whisk in the 2 oz (50 g) castor sugar. Continue whisking until the mixture stands in peaks. Spoon into the soufflé dish on top of the chocolate. Put the dish into a large, deep saucepan (as the pudding will rise spectacularly), with hot water coming three quarters of the way up the sides of the dish. Cover with the lid and cook over the lowest possible heat (the water must not boil or even simmer) for 1$\frac{1}{2}$ hours.

Meanwhile make the sauce. Whisk the egg yolks with the tablespoonful of castor sugar and the brandy. Bring the cream up to the boil and pour it immediately on to the egg yolks, whisking all the time. Leave to cool and then chill in the fridge.

When the pudding is ready, leave it to cool. It will shrink quite a lot, but don't worry, that's normal. Then remove the dish from the pan and chill in the fridge. Shortly before serving carefully loosen the sides with a knife and turn the whole pudding out on to a large serving plate. Some chocolate may still stick to the dish; spoon it out on top of the pudding. Then pour the brandy sauce all round the sides of the pudding and put back in the fridge if not ready to eat at once.

Crunchy Cinnamon Pudding

This is very quick to make and yet good enough for a special occasion. For family meals I make it less rich, and larger, by adding layers of sharp apple purée in between the cream and toasted breadcrumbs.

8 oz fresh breadcrumbs (225 g)
2–3 teaspoonfuls ground cinnamon
3 oz soft dark brown sugar (75 g)
3 oz butter or margarine (75 g)
8 fl oz double or whipping cream (225 ml)
1 oz castor sugar (25 g)
1 carton plain yoghurt

Mix the breadcrumbs, cinnamon and brown sugar together in a bowl. Melt the butter in a large frying pan. Stir in the breadcrumb mixture and fry over a high heat, stirring round all the time with a wooden spoon until the mixture is crisp and toffeeish. Transfer to a plate or bowl and leave to cool. Then whisk the cream until thick. Whisk in the sugar. Stir in the yoghurt. In a serving bowl, 6–7 in (15–18 cm) in diameter, make layers of toasted crumbs and the cream mixture ending with a layer of crumbs. Chill in the fridge before serving.

Entremet Molokoff

I have been unable to find any reason for the name of this luscious pudding. I found the recipe in my grandmother's kitchen notebook and, judging from the menu she has also noted down, it seemed to be her favourite pudding for honoured guests at dinner parties. It certainly is delicious and quick to make too, especially with an electric whisk. Rather like myself, my grandmother hated to waste anything and so used the egg yolks to make a custard to go with the pudding. Personally I think it is better just with a little cream, if anything. You can always use the yolks to enrich a quiche, a cake or a sauce, or of course for mayonnaise.

4 oz granulated sugar (110 g)
8 tablespoonfuls water
3 large egg whites
2 oz castor sugar (50 g)
a few walnuts or hazelnuts—chopped

In a saucepan stir the sugar in 4 tablespoonfuls of the water until dissolved. Then boil over a high heat without stirring for 4–6 minutes until golden brown in colour. Remove from the heat and stir in the other 4 tablespoonfuls of water. Whisk the egg whites until stiff and fold in the castor sugar. Re-heat the caramel to boiling point and pour it slowly in a thin stream on to the egg whites, whisking all the time. (Do this with an electric whisk if possible.) Continue whisking until thick. Put into a round dish and sprinkle the nuts on the top. Chill in the fridge until next day.

Nancy's Nectar

This is an adaptation of an egg-nog recipe given me by an American friend. It is rich, alcoholic and absolutely delicious. Best eaten the day it is made.

3 eggs – separated
4 oz castor sugar (110 g)
finely grated rind of 1 lemon
2 tablespoonfuls brandy
2 tablespoonfuls whisky
¾ pint double cream (425 ml)
½ teaspoonful salt
grated nutmeg

Beat the egg yolks with the sugar and lemon rind in a mixing bowl until thick and lemon-coloured. Gradually beat in the brandy and whisky. Chill in the fridge for at least 1 hour. Whip the cream until stiff and stir lightly into the yolk mixture. Add the salt to the egg whites and whisk until they stand in peaks. Fold into the mixture with a metal spoon. Transfer to a serving dish or into individual dishes and sprinkle with nutmeg. Chill again in the fridge for an hour or more before serving with some thin sweet biscuits.

ICE CREAMS

The majority of ice creams in this chapter are made by a method in which you pour a boiling sugar syrup on to whisking eggs and, having tried several methods, I have found this to be the most successful. It is of course an egg custard base which makes the richest and most creamy ice creams, but it is done rather differently than usual and, as long as you have an electric whisk, more easily. The great advantage is that once you have made your ice cream you just freeze it; no stirring halfway through the freezing – something I never remember to do at the right moment. And the result is just as good as anything made with the most expensive ice cream machine.

Orange Honeycomb Ice Cream

This is more of a chilled pudding than ice cream. It separates while freezing into a light mousse-like top, while the bottom half is like a tangy orange-flavoured caramel. If possible, freeze it in a thick glass dish so that you can see the two layers.

1 large tin evaporated milk
2 eggs
6 oz soft brown sugar (175 g)

6 tablespoonfuls water
1 rounded tablespoonful marmalade
juice of 1 orange

Chill the evaporated milk in the fridge for at least 1 hour before you make the ice cream. Then whisk the eggs until frothy. In not too small a pan, so that it won't boil over, dissolve the sugar in the water over a low heat. Bring to the boil and boil fiercely for 3 minutes. Pour this brown and bubbling syrup in a thin stream on to the eggs, whisking all the time at high speed. Continue whisking until the mixture thickens slightly. Whisk in the marmalade and the orange juice and allow to cool. Then whisk the evaporated milk until thick and whisk in the eggs, sugar and orange mixture. Pour into a fairly deep dish and freeze well.

Rich Banana Ice Cream

What can I say about this ice cream? Smooth as satin, rich as velvet and with the ever-popular flavour of bananas, brown sugar and cream; it's just what a perfect ice cream should be.

3 large eggs
½ teaspoonful salt
6 oz demerara sugar (175 g)
6 tablespoonfuls water

4 bananas
juice of 1 lemon
8 fl oz or ½ pint double or whipping cream (225–275 ml)

Whisk the eggs and salt until frothy. Dissolve the sugar in the water over a low heat, then bring to the boil and boil fiercely without stirring for 3 minutes. Immediately pour this bubbling syrup in a thin stream on to the eggs, whisking all the time as fast as possible. Continue whisking until the mixture thickens. Allow to cool. Then mash the bananas to a purée with the lemon juice and stir into the eggs and sugar. Whisk the cream until thick, not stiff, and stir thoroughly into the mixture. Pour into a dish and freeze.

Strawberry and Lemon Iced Parfait

This rich and creamy ice cream doesn't have to be stirred or whisked halfway through the freezing and can be made using any good fruit purée as a base. Particularly good are blackcurrants, apricots, raspberries or damsons, but if you are using stewed fruit, don't cook them with much sugar.

1 lb fresh or frozen strawberries (450 g)
grated rind and juice of 1 lemon (or
1 small orange)
8 oz castor sugar (225 g)

$\frac{1}{4}$ pint water (150 ml)
2 large egg whites
$\frac{1}{4}$ teaspoonful salt
8 fl oz or $\frac{1}{2}$ pint double or whipping
cream (225–275 ml)

Grate the lemon rind and put on one side. Make a purée of the strawberries with the lemon juice either in a liquidiser or through a sieve. Dissolve the sugar in the water, bring to the boil and boil for 5 minutes. Meanwhile add the salt to the egg whites and whisk until stiff. Pour the hot syrup on to the egg whites in a thin stream, whisking constantly. (This is easiest to do with an electric mixer; if you only have a hand whisk get someone else to pour the syrup while you whisk.) Continue whisking until the mixture is thick. Then lightly stir in the purée and the grated lemon rind. Lastly whip the cream until thick but not stiff and fold it into the mixture with a metal spoon. Pour into a dish and freeze.

Rich Fruit Ice Cream (serves 8)

This wonderfully creamy ice cream can be made with any kind of fruit purée. Sharp strong-flavoured fruits such as apricots (either fresh or dried), plums, blackcurrants or gooseberries are particularly good.

about 1 pint sweetened fruit purée (570 ml)
2 large eggs
½ teaspoonful salt

6 oz castor sugar (175 g)
6 tablespoonfuls water
½ pint double or whipping cream (275 ml)

Make the fruit purée and let it become cold. Whisk the eggs with the salt until frothy. Dissolve the sugar and water in a pan over a low heat. Then boil fiercely without stirring for 3 minutes. Pour the bubbling syrup immediately in a thin stream on to the whisked eggs, whisking all the time at high speed – this is best done with an electric whisk. Continue whisking until the mixture has thickened quite a bit. Whisk in the fruit purée. Then whisk the cream until thick but not stiff and fold thoroughly into the fruit and egg mixture. Pour into a dish and freeze.

Fresh Orange Ice Cream

Very creamy but with a tang of yoghurt, this ice cream is most refreshing and particularly delicious eaten with fresh strawberries.

3 eggs
¼ teaspoonful salt
8 oz granulated sugar (225 g)
¼ pint water (150 ml)

grated rind and juice of
2 small oranges
8 fl oz or ½ pint double or whipping cream (225–275 ml)
1 small carton plain yoghurt

Whisk the eggs with the salt until frothy. Bring the sugar and the water to the boil, stirring to dissolve. Then boil fiercely for 3 or 4 minutes. Immediately pour the syrup in a thin stream on to the eggs, whisking all the time at high speed (ask someone to help you by pouring the syrup if you only have a hand whisk). Continue whisking until the mixture thickens. Whisk the orange juice into the egg mixture and stir in the grated rind. Allow to cool. Then whisk the cream until stiff and stir the yoghurt into it. Give the cooled egg and orange mixture another whisk to amalgamate it and then gently fold in the cream and yoghurt. Pour into a container and freeze.

Fruit and Nut Ice Cream with Port

A luxurious and decorative party ice cream, specially good in winter when there's a lack of fresh fruit. It has a perfect smooth texture and doesn't need beating halfway through the freezing. It is ideal for Christmas festivities.

6 oz currants (175 g)
¼ pint port (150 ml)
4 large eggs
¼ teaspoonful salt
8 oz castor sugar (225 g)
¼ pint water (150 ml)
4 oz shelled walnuts – roughly chopped (110 g)
2 oz chopped candied peel (50 g)
2 oz glacé cherries – roughly chopped (50 g)
½ pint double cream (275 ml)
decoration – a few nuts and halved
glacé cherries and strips of angelica (optional)

Put the currants and port into a saucepan and heat to simmering. Remove from heat and leave until the port is cool. Put the eggs and salt into a mixing bowl and whisk until frothy. Put the sugar and water into a small saucepan. Bring to the boil and boil fiercely for 3 minutes. Immediately pour this mixture in a thin stream into the frothy eggs, while whisking all the time at high speed. (An electric whisk is easiest for this but if you only have a hand one try to get someone else to pour the sugar syrup in while you whisk!) Continue whisking until the mixture thickens and cools. Whip the cream until thick but not stiff. Stir the currants, port, nuts, candied peel and cherries into the cooled egg mixture and lastly fold in the whipped cream. Transfer to a serving bowl and freeze. When frozen decorate with cherries and nuts and cut-out leaves of angelica.

Chocolate Mocha Ice Cream

A rich ice cream, very popular with the children. A more sophisticated version for adults only can be made by adding a little sweet liqueur.

1 tin sweetened condensed milk
3 large eggs
2 tablespoonfuls cocoa

2 teaspoonfuls instant coffee
4 tablespoonfuls warm water
4 tablespoonfuls plain yoghurt

Put the condensed milk into a bowl with the eggs and whisk together. Blend the cocoa and instant coffee in the warm water until smooth and add to the milk and egg mixture. Put the bowl over a pan of simmering water, stirring all the time until the mixture is thick enough to coat the back of a spoon. Remove from the heat and allow to cool. Then stir in the yoghurt, pour into a dish and freeze. The ice cream will be extra creamy if you stir it around once when it is only half frozen.

Rich Chocolate Ice Cream

As its name implies this ice cream is rich and smooth as melted chocolate, and has the advantage of not having to be stirred when half frozen. Perfect for a dinner party, with or without the addition of fruit and nuts.

6 oz plain chocolate (175 g)
3 tablespoonfuls warm water
1 teaspoonful vanilla essence
3 large eggs
¼ teaspoonful salt
5 oz castor sugar (150 g)

6 tablespoonfuls water
4 oz seedless raisins or chopped
nuts or mixture – optional (110 g)
8 fl oz double or whipping
cream (225 ml)

Break the chocolate up and leave to melt with the warm water and vanilla essence in a bowl over a pan of very hot water, stirring once or twice until smooth. Whisk the eggs with the salt until frothy. Put the sugar with the water in a saucepan, bring to the boil and boil fiercely for 3 or 4 minutes. Immediately pour this syrup in a thin stream on to the frothy eggs, while whisking all the time at high speed. (This is easiest with an electric whisk and you may need help if you only have a hand one.) Continue whisking until the mixture thickens. Whisk in the melted chocolate and let the mixture cool completely – this is quicker if you sit the mixing bowl in a sink of cold water. If liked, stir in raisins or nuts. Whip the cream until thick, not stiff and fold into the egg and chocolate mixture. Pour into a container and freeze.

Marshmallow Spice Ice Cream

This is an ice cream for gluttons! It tastes like rich frozen fudge and the children love it. As it's very simple to make it is perfect for holidays.

4 oz packet marshmallows (110 g)
1 large tin evaporated milk
2 teaspoonfuls ground cinnamon

4 oz soft dark brown sugar (110 g)
5–8 fl oz double or whipping cream (150–225 ml)

Melt the marshmallows gently in a pan with the evaporated milk, the spice and the sugar, stirring all the time until smooth. Transfer to a bowl to cool. Then whisk the cream until thick but not stiff and fold thoroughly into the marshmallow mixture. Freeze for at least 3 hours.

Toffee and Hazelnut Ice Cream

I have a childish passion for the taste of toffee and it could hardly be more delicious than in this perfectly smooth-textured ice cream, dotted with crunchy chips of hazelnuts.

4 eggs
$\frac{1}{4}$ teaspoonful salt
8 oz sugar (225 g)
$\frac{1}{4}$ pint water (150 ml)
4 tablespoonfuls warm water

$\frac{1}{4}$ pint double or whipping cream (150 ml)
2–3 tablespoonfuls dark rum (optional)
3–4 oz hazelnuts – chopped (75–110 g)

Whisk the eggs with the salt until frothy. In a saucepan stir the sugar in the $\frac{1}{4}$ pint (150 ml) of water until dissolved, bring to the boil and bubble over a high heat without stirring for 5–6 minutes until golden brown. Don't leave the stove while you are waiting for this to happen as it can turn in a moment to hard, burnt toffee. Remove from the heat and stir in the 4 tablespoonfuls of warm water. Reheat if necessary to boiling point and pour immediately but slowly in a thin stream on to the eggs, beating constantly at high speed. (An electric whisk is obviously much the easiest for this.) Continue beating until the mixture is fairly thick. Allow to cool. (This is quickest if you set the bowl in cold water.) Then whip the cream until thick but not stiff. Stir in the rum if liked. Then fold in the cream and lastly the chopped nuts. Pour into a bowl and freeze at the lowest temperature.

Brown Bread Ice Cream

No one will believe how good this ice cream is until they try it. There have been all sorts of recipes for it from 1860 onwards, but this version is particularly easy to make and doesn't need stirring halfway through the freezing. It is a lovely creamy mixture with the nutty flavour and bite of toasted wholemeal bread incorporated into it.

6 oz fresh wholemeal breadcrumbs (175 g)
½ pint double cream (275 g)
4 oz soft brown sugar (110 g)
6–8 fl oz single cream (175–225 ml)
2 eggs – separated
tablespoonful rum or brandy (optional)

Spread the breadcrumbs in a roasting pan and put in the oven at Gas Mark 5/350°F until crisp and becoming brown – 15–20 minutes. Allow to cool. Whisk the double cream until thick, then thoroughly whisk in the sugar, single cream, egg yolks and rum. Stir in the breadcrumbs. Lastly, whisk the egg whites until stiff and fold into the ice cream mixture. Freeze.

Iced Orange Cups

These are cinnamon-flavoured orange ice creams served in scooped-out fresh orange halves. They look very pretty for a dinner party and taste refreshing after a rich meal.

3 large oranges
4 oz castor sugar (110 g)
½ teaspoonful powdered cinnamon
½ oz or 1 packet powdered gelatine (10 g)
2 tablespoonfuls single cream
3 large eggs – separated
pinch of salt
a spoonful of chopped nuts

Cut the oranges in half, squeeze out the juice and keep the shells on one side. In a double saucepan or a bowl over a pan of simmering water put the sugar, the cinnamon and the gelatine. Strain in the orange juice and stir in the cream. Then stir in the egg yolks, putting the whites aside in a large bowl. Cook over simmering water, stirring constantly with a wooden spoon until the sugar and gelatine have dissolved and the mixture is thick enough to coat the back of the spoon. Pour into a mixing bowl and leave to cool but not set. Scrape any pith out of the orange shells with a teaspoon. Whisk the egg whites with the salt until stiff and fold lightly into the orange custard mixture with a metal spoon. Spoon the mixture into the orange shells, sprinkle with chopped nuts and arrange on a baking sheet or in patty tins which will keep them steady. Put in the freezer or the ice-making part of the fridge for 2–4 hours until frozen.

Fresh Pineapple Sorbet

I think this is one of the most satisfying ices. It is sharp and refreshing, yet the pineapple pulp gives it body which I feel some water ices lack.

8 oz granulated sugar (225 g)
¾ pint water (425 ml)
1 medium to large fresh pineapple

grated rind and juice of 1 lemon
1–2 egg whites

Dissolve the sugar in the water over a low heat. Then bring to the boil and boil, without stirring, for 10 minutes. Leave to get completely cold. Cut the skin off the pineapple, slice and cut out the hard centre bit. Chop the flesh up finely. Mix the flesh and any juice into the cooled syrup with the lemon rind and juice. Pour into a dish and freeze. When half frozen stir round, whisk the egg whites until thick and fold into the mixture. Freeze completely. About an hour before serving put the dish in the non-freezer part of the fridge to allow to soften a bit or to "ripen", as the Italians say.

Old Rectory Water Ice

This ice is made from fresh young blackcurrant leaves which rank with elder flowers for producing the most subtle and scented flavour of early summer. This particular recipe comes from a great friend in Norfolk who has the best kitchen garden I know. All who know it remember each season from year to year by the delights to be eaten from her garden – this blackcurrant leaf water ice is one I particularly look forward to.

1 pint water (570 ml)
8 oz granulated sugar (225 g)

a good handful of fresh
blackcurrant leaves
2 whites of egg

Heat the water and sugar together until dissolved. Then add the blackcurrant leaves. Take the pan off the fire, cover it and leave to infuse overnight or as long as possible. Then strain off the liquid and put in the freezer. Before it completely freezes take it out and stir the mixture round. Whisk the egg whites until stiff and fold into the mixture. Put back in the freezer until frozen.

EXOTIC DELIGHTS

You will see that many of the following recipes use orange or rose flower water. These can be bought at most chemists, and at good grocers and delicatessens. I try to buy the triple strength kind, of which you can use less – half or a third – as in some dishes too much added liquid may make the consistency wrong. Although I have suggested the amount to use it is, of course, a matter of taste, so add the flower water gradually and keep tasting.

For the spices, always buy them whole if you can and, before using, crush them in a small pestle and mortar or a coffee grinder (this may give you wonderfully aromatic coffee next time). Freshly ground spices taste incomparably better, almost a different thing. In fact, I can never believe that the ground nutmeg one buys is the same thing as the whole spice which one grates at home. Cardamom is my very favourite spice, both in sweet and savoury dishes – it also seems to have become the most expensive, but the freshly ground seeds are amazingly pungent so you need very little.

Fried Bananas in Cardamom and Orange Sauce

Fried bananas are absolutely delicious and a very easy pudding, which you can either rustle up at the last minute or make beforehand and keep warm in a low oven.

2 oz unsalted butter (50 g)
6 bananas
4–5 cardamom pods
2 rounded tablespoonfuls soft
brown sugar
juice of 2 large oranges
juice of 1 small lemon
a little brandy, rum or other liqueur (optional)

Melt the butter in a large pan. Peel the bananas and cut them in half lengthways. Fry them very gently in the butter, turning once until soft all through. Remove from the heat and transfer the bananas to a serving dish. Peel the cardamom pods and grind up the seeds with a pestle and mortar. Put the frying pan with the remaining butter in it back on the heat and add the ground cardamom, the sugar and the fruit juice. Bubble over a high heat until slightly reduced and thickened. Then, if liked, add alcohol to taste. Pour the sauce over the bananas and serve with cream.

Baklava

If you live within reach of a Greek shop which sells the ready-made sheets of the paper-thin fila pastry, it is very easy and most worthwhile to make this famous Middle Eastern sweet at home. It is deliciously crisp and light, much better than most baklava bought in Greek restaurants and shops. It doesn't take long to prepare and keeps well for days. And it will certainly impress your friends.

If you have to travel far to buy the fila pastry, it is worth stocking up on it as it keeps indefinitely in the freezer and you can use it for so many things. You can wrap it round almost any kind of sweet or savoury filling (curd or cream cheese is particularly good) making little triangles, rolls or oblongs which you deep fry in hot oil to serve hot or cold. Or you can use several buttered layers of the pastry baked as a topping to a pre-cooked savoury pie. When you buy the pastry wrap it up in polythene until you use it, as if it sits around in the air it becomes dry and brittle and hard to handle.

FOR THE SYRUP
5 oz sugar (150 g)
6 tablespoonfuls water
1 tablespoonful lemon juice
1 tablespoonful rose or orange flower water

FOR THE PASTRY
$\frac{1}{2}$ lb fila pastry (225 g)
4 oz unsalted butter – melted (110 g)
3–4 oz walnuts or sweet almonds – coarsely chopped (75–110 g)
1 tablespoonful sugar

Make the syrup first. Dissolve the sugar in the water and lemon juice over a low heat. Bring to the boil and boil fiercely for 2 minutes to thicken slightly. Remove from the heat and stir in the flower water. Allow to cool and then leave in the fridge.

To make the baklava brush a large (approximately 12 × 8 in (30 × 20 cm), rather shallow, oblong dish with some of the melted butter. Heat the oven to Gas Mark 3/325°F. If your fila pastry is in very large sheets cut it in half. Lay a little under half the sheets in the dish in layers, brushing with melted butter between each layer and folding over the edges if necessary to fit the dish. Then sprinkle over the chopped nuts and the sugar. Lay on and brush with butter the remaining sheets of pastry, buttering the top piece as well. Then, using a sharp knife, cut diagonally across the pastry and then straight downwards making diamond shapes about 2 × 1 in (5 × 2.5 cm). Bake in the centre of the oven for 25–30 minutes then raise the heat to Gas Mark 7/425°F for another 8–10 minutes or until the baklava has become a golden brown. Remove from the oven and pour the cold syrup all over the baklava. Then leave to cool. If you have cooked the baklava in a nice earthenware dish you can simply serve them in that, otherwise cut the pastries out and arrange them in an impressive pile on a pretty serving dish.

Nuri Bey's Fresh Lemon Jelly

This is not a jelly as Britishers know it. The recipe comes from Istanbul and is a smooth, opaque mixture with a wonderfully refreshing sharp lemon flavour.

1¾ pints water (1 litre)
5 oz granulated sugar (150 g)
handful of lemon balm or mint leaves
rind of 2 lemons – peeled off in strips
3 oz cornflour (75 g)
juice of 6 lemons
walnut halves to decorate

Put the sugar, the leaves and the lemon peel into the water and boil up together for 5 minutes. Remove the peel and leaves with a slotted spoon. Blend the cornflour with a little cold water to a smooth paste. Stir it into the hot lemon peel water. Bring to the boil, stirring all the time and bubble for a minute or two until thick. Stir in the juice of 3 lemons and boil for another 2 minutes. Leave until cold and solid. Add the juice of the other 3 lemons and whizz all up in a liquidiser or put through a sieve. Pour into a glass bowl or serving dish and chill well in the fridge. Then decorate the top with the walnuts. Serve with cream.

Muhallabia

This is my easy version of a famous milk pudding from the Middle East. Eaten out of individual pots, its creamy nuttiness and sweetly-scented taste should add an exotic touch to your meal.

1 oz cornflour (25 g)
1¼ pints milk (720 ml)
2 oz castor sugar
2 tablespoonfuls rose water (half as
much if you buy the concentrated kind)
2 oz ground almonds (50 g)

FOR THE SYRUP TOP
5 tablespoonfuls water
4 oz castor sugar (110 g)
1½ tablespoonfuls orange flower
water or rose water
½ oz finely chopped nuts (10 g) – ideally
pistachio but otherwise walnuts or
almonds

Blend the cornflour to a smooth paste with a tablespoonful of the milk. Bring the rest of the milk to boiling point. Stir in the cornflour paste and bring to the boil again. Simmer for 2 or 3 minutes. Add the sugar and the rose water. Stir and cook for a moment more. Stir in the ground almonds. Pour into six small dishes. Allow to cool.

Meanwhile put the water for the syrup in a saucepan and stir in the sugar. Bring to the boil, stirring, and boil for 1 minute. Stir in the orange flower water. Cool slightly and spoon over the cooled Muhallabia. Sprinkle with chopped nuts. Chill for at least 1 hour in the fridge before serving.

Luscious Lychees

Here is an easy way to make a luxuriously exciting creamy jelly out of a simple tin of lychees.

1 large tin (approximately 1 lb 4 oz/560 g) lychees
½ oz or 1 packet gelatine (10 g)
juice of 1 lemon
juice of 1 orange
1 tablespoonful orange flower water
6–8 fl oz double or whipping cream (175–225 ml)
1 heaped tablespoonful demerara sugar
1 oz flaked almonds (25 g)

Drain the juice from the lychees and heat it in a pan. Sprinkle in the gelatine and stir until dissolved. Add the lemon and orange juice and the flower water. Leave until beginning to set, then cut the lychees in half and stir them into the jellying juices. Whisk the cream until thick but not stiff. Fold it only very roughly into the lychee jelly and spoon the mixture in a serving bowl, preferably a pretty glass one. Sprinkle the demerara sugar all over the top – this turns to a syrup in the fridge. Chill well. While the jelly is in the fridge spread the almond flakes on a plate and roast until brown in a medium to high oven for a few minutes. Just before serving scatter the roasted almonds on top of the jelly.

Guava Mousse

Guavas are the cheapest tinned tropical fruit and can make an ordinary fruit salad much more interesting. Even when tinned they retain their good flavour and this is particularly enhanced by the addition of lemon juice. I made this pudding by accident one day because the ingredients were all I had at the time, and the resulting rich and velvety mousse, studded with pink chunks of guava, was a great success.

1 tin guavas
juice of 1 lemon
$\frac{1}{2}$ oz or 1 packet gelatine (10 g)
1 rounded tablespoonful castor sugar
seeds from 1 pod cardamom –
ground in a pestle and mortar (optional)
2 large eggs – separated
5–6 fl oz double or whipping cream (150–175 ml)
pinch of salt

Strain the juice from the guavas and put into a double saucepan or a bowl over a pan of water, together with the lemon juice, gelatine, the sugar, the ground cardamom and the egg yolks. Mix together and then stir over simmering water until the gelatine has dissolved and the mixture has the consistency of a pouring custard. This should not take more than 5–8 minutes. Cut the guava halves in 3–4 pieces and stir them into the custard. Allow to cool. Then whisk the cream until thick and stir the guava mixture into it. Lastly whisk the egg whites with a pinch of salt until stiff and, using a metal spoon, fold into the creamy mixture. Transfer to a serving bowl and chill until set.

Orange and Cardamom Ice Cream with Orange Blossom and Walnut Syrup

Luxurious, creamy ice creams are always a great success, but I think this is the favourite of them all. It is aromatic, rich and creamy, yet still fresh-flavoured. The scented syrup and crunchy nuts give an exciting contrast in texture.

3 large eggs
½ teaspoonful salt
6 oz castor sugar
6 tablespoonfuls water
5–6 cardamom pods
1 can frozen concentrated orange juice
½ pint double or whipping cream (275 ml)

FOR THE SYRUP
4 oz castor sugar (110 g)
4 tablepoonfuls water
2 tablespoonfuls orange flower water
1 tablespoonful lemon juice
1 oz walnuts – roughly chopped (25 g)

First leave the frozen orange juice to thaw a bit. Whisk the eggs with the salt until frothy. Dissolve the sugar in the water over a low heat. Then boil fiercely without stirring for three minutes. Pour the bubbling syrup immediately on to the eggs, whisking all the time at high speed. Continue whisking until the mixture has thickened quite a bit. Remove the seeds from the cardamom pods, crush finely in a pestle and mortar and add to the mixture. Then whisk in the concentrated orange juice thoroughly. Lastly whip the cream until thick but not stiff and fold into the ice cream mixture. Pour into a dish or into a mould and freeze for several hours.

While the ice cream is freezing make the syrup. Dissolve the sugar in the water over a low heat, bring to the boil and boil fiercely for 1 minute. Remove from the heat and stir in the orange flower water and the lemon juice strained through a sieve. Stir in the chopped walnuts and leave to cool. Before serving the ice cream pour the syrup over the top. If you have frozen it in a mould, dip briefly in hot water, turn out on to a serving plate, then pour the syrup over just before putting it on the table.

Rose Petal Water Ice

Roses have not only a good smell but a very definite taste. From the Balkans across to India they add the vital flavour to countless sweet dishes, but here we seem to have forgotten how to use the mass of scented petals which carpet English gardens every summer. Yet rose petal jam stirred into yoghurt is quite as good as the Greek Hymettus honey, and the delicate crystallised petals are both pretty and tasty as a topping for sponge cakes and creamy puddings. They also contrast excellently with the texture of a simple rose petal water ice.

8 oz granulated sugar (225 g)
2 pints water (generous litre)
the petals of 4 scented red or dark pink roses

3–4 drops red food colouring
½–1 tablespoonful rose water
juice of ½ lemon
1–2 egg whites

Dissolve the sugar in the water over a low heat. Then bring to the boil and boil steadily without stirring for 5 minutes. Then lower the heat and add the rose petals. Cover the pan and simmer for another 5 minutes. Leave to cool completely. Then add the food colouring, the rose water and the lemon juice. Pour into a dish and freeze. When half frozen beat to a mush. Whisk the egg whites until thick and fold into the mixture. Freeze again. (If you have any, sprinkle the crystallised petals on top before serving.) Serve with cream.

Crystallised Rose Petals

Petals of 1–2 scented roses
1 large egg white
castor sugar

Simply whisk the egg white until stiff. Dip each petal into it and then into the castor sugar. Lay the petals on a piece of non-stick baking paper on a baking sheet and put low down in the lowest possible oven for 1–1½ hours until quite dry and crisp. Carefully peel the petals off the non-stick paper. Keep in an airtight tin until ready to use.

Rose Petal and Almond Cream

I am almost addicted to the distinctive scented flavour of rose petals. It's satisying to gather them in full, heady bloom just before they drop and even more rewarding when you realise that eating rose petals is not just a romantic idea but a gastronomic delight too.

6 oz granulated sugar (175 g)
½ pint water (275 ml)
petals of 2–4 dark pink or red
scented roses
1 packet or ½ oz gelatine (10 g)
1–2 dessertspoonfuls concentrated
rose water
a squeeze or two of lemon juice
2 oz flaked almonds (50 g)
½ pint double or whipping cream (275 g)

Dissolve the sugar in the water over a low heat. Add the rose petals, bring to the boil, cover and simmer for 10 minutes. Dissolve the gelatine in a little hot water and add to the rose petal mixture. Add the rose water and lemon juice and leave to cool. Spread the almonds on a baking sheet and put in the oven at Gas Mark 4/350°F for 4–6 minutes until golden brown. When the rose petals have nearly set whip the cream until thick and fold thoroughly into the mixture. Stir in three quarters of the roasted almonds. Pour the mixture into a pretty bowl and chill for at least an hour before serving. Just before serving sprinkle the remaining almonds on top.

Kulfi Ice Cream

I first developed a passion for this Indian ice cream in a London restaurant and when I went to India I ate it at every opportunity. It has a concentrated milky and scented flavour which may not be to everyone's taste, but which I love. In India it is laboriously made, as so many of their sweets are, by boiling down fresh milk for hours, stirring all the time. You can avoid this very successfully by using a combination of evaporated and powdered milk. Kulfi ice cream is traditionally served decorated with delicate silver leaf, nuts and often a sweet vermicelli.

1 level tablespoonful ground rice
2 oz full cream powdered milk or
babies' dried milk (50 g)
3 tablespoonfuls hot water
1 large tin evaporated milk
8 fl oz single cream (225 ml)
4 oz castor sugar (110 g)
1 tablespoonful rose water
4—5 cardamom pods – skinned and
the seeds ground to a powder in a
pestle and mortar or a liquidiser
2 oz blanched almonds – chopped (50 g)

Mix the ground rice and powdered milk together to a paste with the hot water. Pour the evaporated milk and cream into a saucepan and bring just to the boil, stirring all the time. Remove from the heat and stir in the rice and milk paste and the sugar. Add the rose water and the ground cardamom seeds. Cool and then freeze in individual dishes. In India they have special pointed moulds for Kulfi ice cream. When frozen I dip the individual dishes briefly in hot water and turn out the ice creams on to a serving dish. Sprinkle with the chopped nuts and serve.

Gulab Jamun

Some of the Indian sweets seem far too sickly for European tastes, but for me there are delicious exceptions. I think these golden milky balls in rose water syrup, with their strange squeaking consistency, are magical.

8 oz full cream powdered milk–I use
St. Ivel Instant Dried Milk (225 g)
1 tablespoonful plain flour
1 tablespoonful baking powder
about ¼ pint milk (150 ml)
sunflower or ground nut oil for deep frying
1 large breakfast cup of sugar
1 large breakfast cup of water
2 tablespoonfuls rose water if you
get the triple strength kind about
3–4 teaspoonfuls only)

Sieve together the milk powder, flour and baking powder. Add enough milk, about ¼ pint (150 ml), to make a stiff dough. Leave to stand for 1 hour, then roll the dough between your palms into walnut-sized balls. Heat the deep oil until only medium hot, not smoking, and deep fry the balls until they expand and are a rich golden brown all over. The oil must not get too hot or the balls will become brown too quickly and won't cook properly inside. Drain the balls on some absorbent paper or a cloth. Meanwhile make a syrup by boiling the sugar and water fiercely for 2 or 3 minutes and then adding the rose water. Put the balls into a bowl (they look beautiful in a pretty glass bowl) and pour the hot syrup over them. Allow to soak for a few hours before serving.

SAVOURIES

Camembert Ice Cream

This unusual iced savoury is excellent and very quick to prepare.

3 oz ripe camembert – with the skin
trimmed off (75 g)
1 tablespoonful top of the milk
½ pint double cream (275 ml)

salt, black pepper, cayenne pepper
a few lettuce leaves
oat cakes or wafer biscuits

Mash the camembert, which should be at room temperature, and the top of the milk together with a fork as smoothly as possible. Whisk the cream until thick and then whisk the mashed camembert thoroughly into the cream. Season with plenty of black pepper and salt. Put the mixture into a shallow rectangular dish and sprinkle the top with a little cayenne pepper. Before serving take out of the freezer and leave out for 5–10 minutes to soften a little. Then cut the ice cream into fingers and arrange on a bed of lettuce leaves. Serve with hot oat cakes or water biscuits.

French Bacon Fingers

I had these first in a Parisien pâtisserie and found that they were extremely simple to copy, using bought puff pastry. They are very light and good as a savoury or as something tasty to nibble with drinks. However, when I make them they often don't last that long as the children consume them within minutes of getting in from school! A good alternative is to fill the pastry fingers with anchovies or anchovy paste instead of the bacon.

8 oz packet puff pastry (225 g)
approximately 8 oz streaky bacon
with the rinds cut off (225 g)
1 egg yolk

Cut the pastry in half and roll out into two rectangles about ⅛ in (3 mm) thick. Lay the bacon rashers close together on one rectangle, then lay the other piece of pastry on top and press down all over. Using a very sharp knife cut into fingers about ¾ × 2½ in (2 × 6 cm). Heat the oven to Gas Mark 6/400°F. Grease a large baking sheet and arrange the fingers on it. Brush them with the egg yolk and cook just above the centre of the oven for 10–15 minutes until puffed up and golden brown. Serve warm or cold.

JDBOP—7 **

Stuffed Cheese Shortbreads

These light crunchy biscuits sandwiched together with a creamy cheese and chive mixture make a tempting end to the meal. You can make the biscuits long in advance and keep them in an airtight tin, and of course eat them by themselves too.

FOR THE SHORTBREADS
6 oz plain flour (175 g)
1 teaspoonful salt
3 oz fine semolina (75 g)
4 oz strong cheddar cheese – grated finely (110 g)
6 oz butter – at room temperature (175 g)

FOR THE FILLING
6 oz cream cheese (175 g)
1 heaped tablespoonful
chopped fresh chives,
spring onions or parsley
black pepper

Heat the oven to Gas Mark 2/300°F. Lightly grease a large baking sheet or tin. Mix the flour, salt and semolina together in a bowl. Add the cheese and butter. Work the mixture together thoroughly with your fingers until you have a smooth dough. Roll out thickly – about $\frac{1}{4}$ in ($\frac{1}{2}$ cm) on a floured board and cut into small biscuits with a 2 in (5 cm) cutter. Arrange on the baking sheet and bake in the centre of the oven for 1 hour. Allow to cool a little and then transfer the biscuits to a wire tray until cold. To make the filling simply soften the cream cheese with a fork and mix in the chopped chives and black pepper to taste. Use to sandwich together the biscuits.

Bacon and Mustard Sticks

These crumbly sticks are a good accompaniment when you are finishing your meal with cheese. The addition of wholemeal flour gives a nutty flavour.

4 oz streaky bacon rashers (I prefer
smoked) (110 g)
2 oz butter or margarine (50 g)
2 oz plain white flour (50 g) ⎫ or 3 oz plain white flour (75 g)
1 oz wholemeal flour (25 g) ⎭
1 rounded teaspoonful baking powder
salt, black pepper
1 egg yolk
1 teaspoonful mustard
2 teaspoonfuls water

Cut the rind off the bacon and bake in the oven at Gas Mark 5/375°F for 15–20 minutes until crisp. Allow to cool a little and then crumble. Melt the butter over a low heat. Leave to cool a little. Mix the flours, baking powder, salt and pepper together in a bowl. Drop in the egg yolk, the crumbled bacon, the mustard and the water. Gradually mix in the melted butter with a wooden spoon. When thoroughly mixed, flour your hands and gather the mixture up into a ball. Wrap in a little foil or polythene and leave in the fridge for at least 30 minutes. Heat the oven to Gas Mark 7–425°F and butter a baking sheet. Take little pieces of dough in your hands and roll between your palms into thin sticks, 2½–3 in (6–7.5 cm) long. Arrange the sticks on the baking sheet and bake towards the top of the oven for 8–10 minutes.

Brown Bread Cheese Rolls

This is just what a savoury should be – simple to make but titillating to the palate. Sometimes I make these rolls for my children's high tea – they love them.

3 oz grated cheese (75 g)
1 teaspoonful Worcestershire sauce
pinch of cayenne pepper
1 large egg – beaten

6 thin sliced large slices of brown bread
2 oz melted butter (50 g)
a few sprigs of parsley (optional)

Lightly butter a shallow ovenproof dish. Mix the grated cheese in a bowl with the Worcestershire sauce, the cayenne and the beaten egg. Cut the crusts off the bread. Spread the cheese mixture on to the slices and roll up. Arrange the rolls in a dish and brush with half the melted butter. Put under a low to medium grill for about 5 minutes unitl golden brown – then turn the rolls over, brush again with the rest of the butter and grill until the second side is also browned and crisp. Garnish with sprigs of parsley and serve.

Crispy Cheese Roll

This is a savoury Swiss roll made with pastry and is good after a light meal or as a supper or lunch dish with a salad. Using packet puff pastry it is very quick to prepare.

8 oz puff pastry (225 g)
8 oz cottage cheese (225 g)
6 oz grated cheese (175 g)
1 teaspoonful dried oregano or fresh herbs or grated nutmeg

salt, black pepper
1 egg – lightly whisked
milk or egg yolk for the glaze
a little grated parmesan or sesame seeds

Heat oven to Gas Mark 7/425°F. Roll out the pastry into a rectangle approximately 8 × 10 in (20 × 25.5 cm). Prick all over with a fork. Put the cheeses, herbs or nutmeg, seasoning and egg into a bowl and mix together thoroughly. Spread the mixture on to the pastry within ½ in (1 cm) of the edges. Moisten the edges. Roll up loosely and press the ends together like a parcel. Put on to a greased baking sheet and brush with milk or egg yolk. Make slashes along the top of the roll at 1 in (2.5 cm) intervals and sprinkle with parmesan or sesame seeds. Bake towards the top of the oven for 20–30 minutes until the pastry is risen and rich golden brown.
the oven on a damp baking tray for 20–30 minutes until the pastry is risen and rich golden brown.

Cockle Coriander Cases

Using the frozen uncooked vol-au-vent cases, these are very easy and economical to make up either as a savoury or as a first course. The stuffing has a creamy nutty flavour, more exciting than the usual bland vol-au-vent fillings.

1 frozen packet uncooked vol-au-vent cases (12 medium size)
¼ pint double or whipping cream (150 ml)
2 teaspoonfuls ground coriander

2 teaspoonfuls fresh or dried dill or chives
4 oz cockles (110 g)
2 oz button mushrooms – sliced thinly (50 g)
salt, black pepper

Cook the vol-au-vent cases according to the instructions and allow to cool. Whip the cream until thick but not stiff. Then simply stir in the other ingredients in the order given, seasoning with salt and black pepper to taste. Pile this filling into the vol-au-vent cases. Keep in a cool place but not the fridge, until ready to serve.

Aubergine Purée

If you have a liquidiser, this most dreamy Turkish speciality is no trouble to make but tastes as if you have laboured for hours. It has a distinctive smoky flavour and makes an unusual savoury or first course which people ask for again and again. The purée will keep for days in a covered container in the fridge.

2 medium sized roundish aubergines – about ¾ lb (350 g)
juice of ½ lemon
3–4 tablespoonfuls sunflower seed oil

salt, black pepper
chopped parsley to garnish
brown toast

Put the aubergines unpeeled under a very hot grill, turning them once or twice until the skin is black and beginning to blister. This will probably take 10–15 minutes. Peel off the skin – as they will be hot this is easiest to do under cold water. Then put them in a large sieve and press down with a wooden spoon or a plate to squeeze as much juice as possible out of them. Now they will look unappetisingly like old rags, but a wonderful transformation is about to take place! Put them in the liquidiser with the lemon juice and whizz up, adding the sunflower oil a little at a time until the mixture is smooth, pale and very light. Add salt and pepper to taste. Put into a serving bowl, decorate with chopped parsley and chill for thirty minutes or more before serving with thin brown toast.

Herring and Apple in Soured Cream

The trouble with hot savouries is that most of them were created in the days when nearly all households had a cook. Nowadays, it's just possible to leap up from the table and put a prepared dish into the oven or under the grill for a few minutes but it's much more relaxing to know that everything is already done leaving you free to enjoy the meal as much as your guests. This delicious dish, which can be either a savoury, a first course or eaten as a cold lunch in summer, takes only minutes to prepare.

**2–3 pickled herring fillets – 5–6 oz
(150–175 g)
1 small onion
1 firm eating apple
1 carton soured cream
$\frac{1}{4}$ of a whole nutmeg – grated
salt, black pepper
garnish – chopped fresh mint,
chives or parsley**

Rinse the fish thoroughly under cold water and pat dry. Cut the fillets into small pieces. Peel the onion and slice into very fine rounds. Peel the apple and cut into small thin pieces. Mix these ingredients with the soured cream, adding the grated nutmeg with salt and black pepper to taste. Transfer the mixture to a serving dish and sprinkle with the chopped fresh mint.
Serve the same day with thin brown bread.

SAUCES AND BISCUITS

Bay Tree Custard

This light egg custard, subtly flavoured with bay leaf, is well worth making. It is something quite different from packet custard and quite delicious poured over hot pies, tarts and steamed puddings. Or for a simple and extremely popular dessert slice some bananas into a bowl, mix with a little brown sugar and lemon juice and then stir in the custard.

2 large eggs
1 bay leaf
a little more than ½ pint milk (275 ml)
½ teaspoonful vanilla essence
1 rounded tablespoonful castor sugar

Lightly whisk 1 whole egg and 1 yolk (reserving the white) in a bowl. Add the bay leaf to the milk in a saucepan and bring to the boil. Remove from the heat, take out the bay leaf and pour the hot milk on to the eggs, whisking all the time. Add the vanilla essence and sugar. Pour back into the saucepan. Stir with a wooden spoon over a gentle heat until the custard thickens just enough to coat the back of the spoon. This shouldn't take long but you must be careful not to let it boil at all. (If it should go slightly lumpy, just whisk again thoroughly and even if it curdles, all is not lost, whizz it in a liquidiser for a moment until smooth again.) Let the custard cool. Then whisk the reserved egg white until stiff and fold gently but thoroughly into the custard. Chill in the fridge before serving.

Hot Chocolate and Orange Sauce

This is a luscious sauce to pour over either vanilla or chocolate ice cream, and it couldn't be simpler to make.

3 tablespoonfuls golden syrup
2 oz butter (50 g)
3 oz plain chocolate (75 g)
juice of 1 large orange

Simply put all the ingredients in a pan and heat gently. Stir until the chocolate has melted and the sauce is smooth.

Hot Raspberry and Orange Sauce

A quick sauce, very popular with children, to go with vanilla ice cream and milk puddings.

4 rounded tablespoonfuls raspberry jam
juice of 2 oranges
1 rounded teaspoonful cornflour
2 tablespoonfuls water
juice of 1 small lemon

Press the jam through a sieve into a saucepan to free it from all seeds. Melt the jam in the orange juice over a low heat. Dissolve the cornflour in the water and stir into the sauce. Bring to the boil, stirring, and bubble gently for 2 minutes. Turn off the heat and add the lemon juice. Pour into a jug and serve hot.

Chilled Brandy Sauce

This quickly made, light and creamy sauce is delicious with almost any hot pudding, and can also be an alternative to brandy butter with Christmas pudding.

¼ pint double cream (150 ml)
1 level tablespoonful icing sugar – sifted
1–2 tablespoonfuls brandy

Simply whisk the cream until thick, then whisk in the icing sugar and gradually stir in the brandy to taste. Chill in the refrigerator.

Brandy Butter

For most children a huge dollop of rum or brandy butter is the only reason that they will eat a bit of the Christmas pudding. You can make the butter when you make the pudding, pack it into a plastic box with a lid and store it in your refrigerator. Take out well beforehand on Christmas Day.

8 oz unsalted butter (225 g)
4—6 oz (to taste) sugar (110–175 g)
4—5 tablespoonfuls brandy

Cream the butter until pale and soft. Beat in the sugar. Add the brandy drop by drop, beating all the time so that it doesn't curdle.

Rum Butter

8 oz unsalted butter (225 g)
4—6 oz (to taste) soft, pale brown
sugar (110–175 g)
4—5 tablespoonfuls light rum

Cream the butter until pale and soft. Beat in the sugar. Add the rum drop by drop, beating all the time so that it doesn't curdle.

Crème Fraîche

Outside France it's difficult to find this slightly sharp, refreshing cream but here's a quick version to make at home.

¼ pint double cream (150 ml)
1 dessertspoonful plain yoghurt

Simply stir the cream and yoghurt together and chill.

Orange Butter Finger Biscuits
(for eating with ice cream)

These are a version of the American refrigerated biscuits where a rich, soft dough is formed into a roll and chilled well in the fridge before being sliced thinly and baked. It's so convenient. This amount of dough will make at least three batches of about thirty small biscuits – you just keep it in the fridge and slice as much as you like whenever you want to produce deliciously crisp, light biscuits within 10 minutes. They are a perfect accompaniment to all kinds of ice cream and other creamy puddings but irresistible at any time.

7 oz castor sugar (200 g)	**grated rind of 1 orange**
4 oz butter (110 g)	**8 oz strong plain flour (225 g)**
1 large egg	**½ teaspoonful salt**
1 teaspoonful vanilla essence	**2 teaspoonfuls baking powder**

Beat the butter and sugar until light and creamy. Thoroughly beat in the egg. Add the vanilla essence and the orange rind. Sift the flour with the salt and baking powder and stir into the butter and egg mixture. Flour your hands and shape the dough into a long, rather flat roll (so that the sliced off biscuits will be finger shaped – they expand while cooking). If you find the dough too soft to shape, chill it until it is manageable. Wrap the roll up in plastic or foil and chill for at least 12 hours, more if possible.

To cook, heat the oven to Gas Mark 5/375°F and have ready a large baking tray. Take the roll of dough from the fridge and, using a sharp knife, slice off the biscuits as thinly as possible and arrange on the baking tray. Bake in the centre of the oven for 7–9 minutes until a pale golden colour. Immediately, while the biscuits are hot, ease off carefully with a palette knife. If you can resist eating them all at once keep them in an airtight container.

Barbados Biscuits

Rich shortbread biscuits with the flavour of dark, moist sugar from the West Indies. Perfect to accompany a plain vanilla ice cream, or an apricot fool.

7 oz butter (200 g)
2 oz soft dark brown Muscovado
sugar (50 g)
½ lb self-raising flour (225 g)

Heat the oven to Gas Mark 5/375°F. Cream the butter and sugar together thoroughly. Work in the flour with your fingers. Gather into a ball and knead lightly, flouring your hands if the mixture is hard to handle. Roll out on a floured board about ¼ in (½ cm) thick and cut into rounds with the rim of a glass or a fluted cutter. Re-roll as necessary. Lay the rounds on lightly greased baking sheets and bake in the centre of the oven for 7–8 minutes. Don't let the biscuits become too brown. Let them cool on the tray.

Almond Biscuits (makes about 30 little biscuits)

These are small, light biscuits perfect as an accompaniment to ice cream and fruit fools.

2 sheets rice paper
2 large egg whites
2 oz icing sugar (50 g)

2 oz ground almonds (50 g)
1 heaped teaspoonful cornflour
a few flaked almonds

Heat the oven to Gas Mark 2/300°F. Lay the rice paper on a large baking sheet. Whisk the egg whites until they stand in soft peaks. Sieve the icing sugar into a bowl and mix in the ground almonds and cornflour. Fold the mixture gently but thoroughly into the egg whites. Spoon rounded teaspoonfuls of the mixture on to the rice paper – they will hardly spread during the cooking so they can be fairly close together. Lay a piece of flaked almond on top of each biscuit. Cook in the centre of the oven for 20–25 minutes until pale brown round the edges. Allow to cool and then tear off the rice paper surrounding each biscuit. Store in an airtight container.

Index